7 776269 56

D1494593

Praise f

For Roxanne

Dubai Dreams

Inside the Kingdom of Bling

Raymond Barrett

NICHOLAS BREALEY
PUBLISHING

LONDON · BOSTON

First published by
Nicholas Brealey Publishing in 2010

3–5 Spafield Street
Clerkenwell, London
EC1R 4QB, UK
Tel: +44 (0)20 7239 0360
Fax: +44 (0)20 7239 0370

20 Park Plaza
Boston
MA 02116, USA
Tel: (888) BREALEY
Fax: (617) 523 3708

www.nicholasbrealey.com
www.raymondbarrett.com

ISBN: 978-1-85788-527-9

British Library Cataloguing in Publication Data
A catalogue record for this book is available from the
British Library.

Illustrations © Niall Flaherty 2010
Cover design Ken Leeder
Front cover image www.mukks.com
Back cover image © Fabrice Bettex / Alamy

FSC
Mixed Sources
Product group from well-managed
forests and other controlled sources

Cert no. SGS - COC - 2061
www.fsc.org
© 1996 Forest Stewardship Council

Printed in the UK by Clays St Ives plc
on Forest Stewardship Council certified paper.

Contents

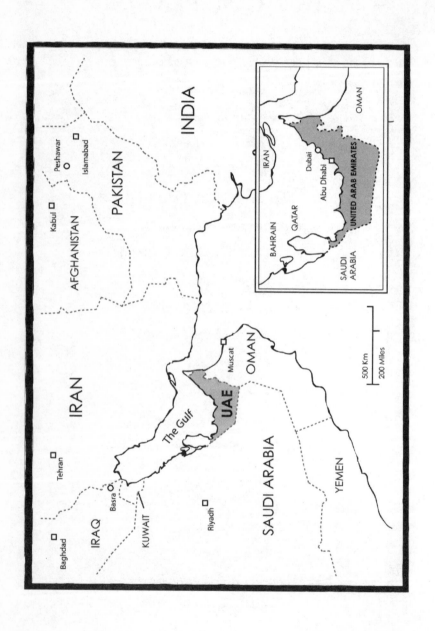

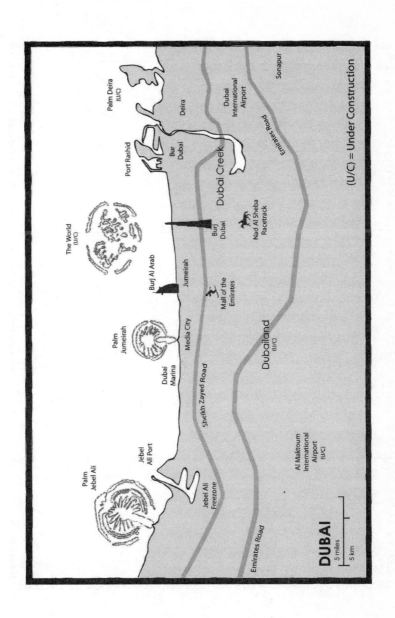

DUBAI

5 miles
5 km

Palm Jebel Ali

Jebel Ali Port

Jebel Ali Freezone

Palm Jumeirah

Dubai Marina

Media City

The World (U/C)

Burj Al Arab

Jumeirah

Sheikh Zayed Road

Mall of the Emirates

Dubailand (U/C)

Al Maktoum International Airport (U/C)

Emirates Road

Port Rashid

Bur Dubai

Burj Dubai

Nad Al Sheba Racetrack

Palm Deira (U/C)

Deira

Dubai Creek

Dubai International Airport

Emirates Road

Sonapur

(U/C) = Under Construction

Prologue: The Kingdom of Bling

THE AIR IS CRISP, DRY, AND COLD and everyone is wrapped up in hats and gloves. Snowboarders whistle past unsteady skiers freshly graduated from the bunny slopes, still learning the basics of movement and motion in this white other world. A young woman wearing a *hejab* (or headscarf) in keeping with the local understanding of Islamic modesty slaloms past me, while a gaggle of young children shriek and screech as they toboggan down a slide, experiencing the thrill of snow for the first time. Outside it's nearly 120 degrees Fahrenheit. By nightfall the city will be transformed into a pressure cooker, but inside on these powdery slopes, cocooned from the sand and the heat, the limits of the natural world are momentarily forgotten.

This is Dubai: a place where the confines of the imagination no longer apply. The ski slope I have just descended is the centerpiece of the expansive Mall of the Emirates. Behind huge glass windows, a rainbow of nationalities stand and rubberneck in shorts and t-shirts, marveling at the incongruity of it all. The contrasts couldn't be more elemental: warmth and fire against cold and ice; desert sand juxtaposed with snow slopes. In much of Arabia, though affluence may be displayed through gold and diamonds, true wealth is expressed by a somewhat cavalier attitude toward the region's most precious substance: water. And if fountains and waterfalls are the playthings of the rich and powerful, snow is the ultimate accessory in this futuristic kingdom of bling.

Despite humble beginnings, Dubai is now a superlative city. Within its municipal borders you can find constructions with global ambitions: the tallest building in the world, the largest shopping mall, the most luxurious hotel. In less than a generation, a once diminutive port town has transformed itself into an instantly recognizable brand, synonymous with wealth and luxury.

Nevertheless, in the decade in which I was living in and traveling round the Arab world, the "real" Middle East seemed to lie elsewhere. The stories that inevitably attracted the attention and interest of the world at large were generally of a less aspirational nature: suicide bombers (Israel, Iraq, Saudi Arabia), politically inspired shootings and bombings (Egypt, Kuwait, Jordan), sectarian strife and ethnic tensions (Turkey), political assassinations (Syria, Lebanon), regime change, civil war, sectarian strife, beheadings, and kidnappings (Iraq), nuclear tensions (Iran), one-party totalitarian states (Syria), all-out war (Israel–Lebanon), internecine strife and mass civilian slaughter (Gaza). Since the Second World War the Middle East has been more famous for discord than harmony, as revolutions, religious and ethnic conflict, postcolonial dissension, and imperial chicanery have defined the region.

But Dubai didn't fit this picture. Here was a point on the regional map that had distinguished itself from the surrounding countries and defined itself in different terms: a place of peace amid war; a place of enterprise amid stagnation; a place of action amid torpidity; a place of permissiveness amid a region prone (of late at least) to restriction; a place of optimism where pessimism is often the pervading mood. Here was something else to explore: a Middle Eastern success story that defied expectations, and one that was based on innovation and risk taking rather than oil reserves. While the region had been tarred with the brush of failure, regression, and intolerance, Dubai heralded itself as a center of success, progress, and inclusivity. Such an upbeat message was a different story to tell.

Despite its tempestuous location, Dubai has been steadfast in ignoring the age-old adage that you must learn to

2

walk before you can run. It took a seat at the world table with what little stake it had and asked to be dealt a hand. The fact that one of their own had the grand intention to reinvent itself invoked both incredulity and a certain degree of mirth among many of its Middle Eastern neighbors. Undeterred, Dubai forged ahead and exhausted billions upon billions of dollars to remake itself in an image of its own creation – a place where opulence and growth were the norm, rather than the exception. While the rest of the Arab world was still learning how to walk, Dubai learned how to ski.

It is clear that you are sitting down with a high roller even before your plane touches down at Dubai International Airport. Arriving at night there is at first little sign of life below, except for the occasional bursts of orange flames coming from the oil fields of Saudi Arabia and Abu Dhabi. If you could peel away the blackness, a harsh landscape would reveal itself. The coastline along the eastern shores of the Arabian peninsula is a sparse, gravelly place with little of the grandeur one associates with a classic desert scene. But suddenly, the emptiness below is lit up by a vast swathe of yellow and orange halogen, spreading for miles out into the desert. From high up in the sky Dubai looks like a giant pinball machine, a mass of geometric shapes and luminous grids stretching out into the blackness beyond.

One of the first things you can see is the outline of a palm-shaped archipelago glowing out of the night-time waters of the Arabian Gulf. This is the Palm Jumeirah, a five kilometer-wide artificial island containing luxury resorts and celebrity-endorsed villas. By superimposing this quintessential image of Old Arabia onto the Gulf, Dubai shows that it doesn't hang about when introducing itself to visitors. In doing so, the humble palm tree has been turned into a globally recognized corporate logo – a Nike swoosh with representation at the United Nations.

Yet politically Dubai has somewhat of an identity crisis, as it is neither simply a city, nor even a country in its own right. Along with the six other emirates (Abu Dhabi, Sharjah, Ajman, Um Al Quwain, Ras Al Khaimah, and Fujairah), Dubai is but one of seven self-governing entities constituting the United Arab Emirates, which came into being after the British called time on a mixed bag of protectorates along the Arabian Gulf in 1971. The UAE federal government takes care of the boring stuff, such as printing currency, issuing passports, buying F-16 fighter aircraft from Washington, or establishing diplomatic relations with the now-defunct Islamic Emirate of Afghanistan (aka the Taliban). Day to day, each of the emirates functions independently, somewhat like Texas and Florida, just without the democracy. Each emirate has its own absolute ruler and ruling family, governs according to its own laws, and, most importantly, tots up its own balance sheet. It's only when dealing with the outside world that the heptet try to act as a collective.

In the midst of these politically ambiguous entities you find Dubai, which over the years has undergone a transubstantiation that even a Jesuit priest would find difficult to explain. Two centuries back there was barely anything here at all, as the founding of the city-state dates to the 1830s, when the seedling of what the world knows as Dubai was planted. Advance a hundred years and there was still barely any resemblance to what one sees today: as the Manhattan skyline rose up over New York to a jazz beat in the 1920s, what little wealth Dubai possessed was measured simply in date trees, camels, and other livestock. Even as Elvis was recording "That's All Right (Mama)," the majority of Dubai's inhabitants still lived in *barasti* houses made from palm trees; only a select few could enjoy the comforts of a home made from mud. The first concrete building did not appear until the 1950s. However, fast forward to the present day and the picture alters beyond recognition. Now around two million people live where there were 50,000 a generation before.

Exactly how such a transformation could have occurred so quickly has engendered a great deal of debate. After all, Dubai is one of the United *Arab* Emirates, which has not exactly been a byword for rapid-fire growth (at least not in the last millennium). *Shwaya, shwaya, habibi, bukhara, inshallah* (take it easy, take it easy, my dear, tomorrow, God willing) is a phrase you can hear regularly across the region as you try to accomplish the most basic of everyday tasks, be it getting a phone line installed or applying for a driver's license. A less literal translation of that ubiquitous Arabic phrase could be rendered thus: "What's the rush, my friend? This will get done at some undetermined point of time in the future, and in the end, we know it's out of my control anyway and in the hands of the Big Man upstairs." Dubai's breakneck (some would say blitzkrieg) approach to development seemed to make a mockery of the stereotype.

It is important to understand that despite the fact that many of its neighbors sit on vast reserves of petroleum and gas, Dubai's own oil reserves are rather paltry and account for only around 5 percent of its economy. So Dubai's rise from a flyspeck on the map of the Middle East to global prominence is no mere whimsy on the part of some oil-rich sheikh. When a New Yorker flies to Singapore via Dubai on Emirates Airways, or an English football fan cheers his team at the Emirates Stadium in London, little do they realize that they are part of a master plan conceived by Dubai's ruling family and a coterie of international consultants. The aim was grand but simple: to make the city the premier playground of the Middle East, Central and South Asia (over two billion potential customers) – a place where extravagance is standard and affluence is accessible by all.

The first step involved attracting tourists, travelers, expatriates, entrepreneurs, multinational corporations, and money from all over the world. By allowing all of these disparate elements to coexist, a global hub of entertainment for finance and trade would also be created. The merchants of cliché went into overdrive and the "Dubai dream" was born: a point of engagement between East and West and existing in the imagination as much as on a map. The second step involved the biggest building boom the region had seen since Nebuchadnezzar built his *ziggurat* in Babylon over 2,000 years ago. As Dubai charged down a path of superlative development, it forced itself on the world's collective unconscious and transformed from a Middle Eastern Monaco into a global, Arabian-themed Disneyworld.

When it came to marketing the Dubai dream, subtlety was out and bling was most definitely in. Even a superstructure such as Burj Dubai – the tallest building in the world – was only a pinprick in an unrestrained outpouring of concrete and glass. On the outskirts of the city, ground was broken on the three billion square foot Dubailand, modestly self-styled as "the world's most ambitious tourism, leisure and entertainment project." Projected to be three times bigger than Manhattan and more than twice the size of the city of Dubai itself, the publicists insisted that this friendly little funfair would include re-creations of the Hanging Gardens of Babylon, the Taj Mahal, and the Eiffel Tower. Yet this was not wanton gigantism. The secret to good advertising is repetition and the public relations experts knew what it took to set the media quacking. Since this rebranding exercise was targeted at a global audience, its message had to be clear. And Dubai's elevations of architecture speak an Esperanto of aspiration, easily understood across every continent.

Today, a flight to Dubai is a pilgrimage that millions make each year. Gulf Arabs and Iranians come to escape the restrictions imposed by their own rulers on alcohol and other entertainments. European tourists fly in for sun served with a dollop of luxury. Central Asian shoppers enter on business and leave with a host of consumer goods unavailable at home. Expatriates from India arrive to work and find a richer life, while long-haul travelers stop over for a few days on their way from continent to continent. And all of Dubai's aspirations are made clear as soon you land. As you pass through the terminal building, a host of advertisements sing the emirate's praises, insisting that this is the ultimate place to live in the twenty-first century. On one occasion, as I stood in line at passport control, the large illuminated sign overhead carried a message of such brazen conviction that I wanted to believe it: "WELCOME TO THE FUTURE."

However, a dream can't last for ever. Despite the optimism in which Dubai trades, skeptics insist that a hard rain is going to fall. Even though Dubai imagines itself a gilded Prospero's island free from the restrictions of time and place, the city's rapid descent down the black runs of the global economy has come with complications. The Dubai dream was built on a tsunami of borrowed money and this in turn fueled a property bubble of epic proportions, which finally popped with a resonance that left the city reeling. The city's fabled cranes ground to a juddering halt and many of the emirate's more ambitious projects were mothballed indefinitely. Liquidity concerns soon morphed into solvency issues as the Dubai state-owned companies building the dream fell behind on their debts. Across the city's new high-rise suburbia (which sprouted to life in less than a decade) forests of apartment buildings stood idly by, still in search of elusive end-users. Though the high-reaching skylines of Shanghai and Mumbai shout similar aspirations, these were a result and a reflection of economic virility. Dubai, on the other hand, used construction as a means to growth, a model of development that has since been deemed rather reckless.

Given its lack of modesty, people generally have pugilistic impressions of Dubai that only come in black or white. In one corner you have the champions: the ruling family, the local privileged élite, property developers, marketing professionals, investment bankers, businessmen, architectural and interior design futurists, and a range of others keen to enjoy the social freedoms on offer. Supporters are impressed by the ambition and audacity of it all. This is a place that has prospered on guile and gumption rather than oil and gas. In the past, Dubai had merely regional ambitions: to be a weekend escape from Saudi Arabia for those in need of wine with dinner or bacon for breakfast. But Dubai's more recent neophytes have a much broader perspective. To these people, the emirate is a place for those who "have" rather than those who "have not," and thus there will always be a market for what it has to offer.

In the other corner you find an unlikely alliance of detractors: Islamic fundamentalists and western human rights advocates, environmentalists and traditionalists, socialists and libertines, who perceive only Pyrrhic victories in the successes achieved so far. Cultural purists see a mongrelized abomination of its former self. Repulsed, these critics insist that Dubai embodies the very worst instincts of humankind: hubris, gluttony, and inequality. They see consumption without production and the dominance and glorification of materialism over the natural world. Only in Dubai would a developer announce proudly to the world that the cooling system in his latest project had the chilling power of 10,000,000 kilograms of *melting* ice per day. Skeptics maintain that the Dubai dream is unsustainable and envision a lost kingdom of ghostly superstructures, a hurriedly built Araby bazaar standing empty and idle in the desert.

During my time exploring the city, I experienced a place that did not fit the one-dimensional portraits painted by either the braying jackals of doom or the hear-no-evil, see-no-evil publicity reps. It was ridiculous to speak of it as a single entity, despite the convenience of these opposing narratives. The Dubai dream was merely an abstraction, something that would always feel intangible. My experience showed me something else: a place defined by people, not by conceits or assaults; as likely to engender ethical schizophrenia as moral certainty. Though Gulf Arabs flock in droves to its bespangled emporiums of consumption, they also acknowledge that the city's infatuation with earthly pleasures is "against Islam."

Here was a plurality whose worth could not be measured in dirhams or dinars; here were dreams that would hold their value, regardless of any fluctuations in the market. The questions I sought to answer were not so readily quantifiable and the answers resonated more deeply than property prices. What was it really like to live in a city that used exclamation marks to punctuate every aspect of itself? Was there any substance to the claims of prosperity, dynamism, and success? Where were the intersections of experience that would ultimately lead to a true understanding of this place? And who were the people who fleshed out the stories that gave life to the dream, behind the brilliance, the bluster, and the bling?

1

Dubai Dreams

EVERY CITY HAS ITS DEMARCATION LINES, both physical and figurative, which evolve over time and leave their own unique impressions on the land. Water, invariably, adds the most definition. For example, in Dublin you are either a Northsider or a Southsider, depending on which side of the river Liffey you were born. Those born north of the river will spend a lifetime being portrayed as a little rough around the edges, while those who hail from the "south side" are seen as soft, moneyed, and somehow British, by far the worst possible slur against one's character in Ireland. Dubai is little different in this regard. The city is cleft in two by the Creek, an inlet of the Persian Gulf that winds inland in a lazy S for more than six miles. On its journey the Creek passes a number of landmarks: a former

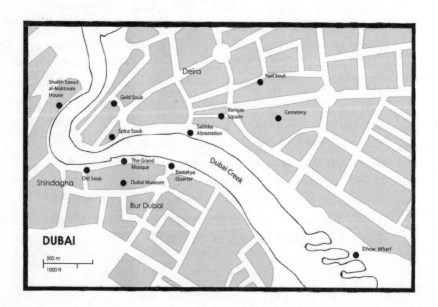

royal abode, restored period houses, glass-fronted high-rise hotels, and a golf club, before finally putting up its feet amid a wildlife sanctuary that plays host each year to flocks of migrating flamingos. The meandering course the Creek follows is a history lesson of sorts, charting the city's rise from an anonymous pearl-diving port to a regional trade center, and from there to a global financial and entertainment hub.

Orientation in any new city can be a challenge but in Dubai the matter is straightforward: once you know where you stand in relation to the Creek, you know where you are in Dubai. The Creek laid the foundation of the modern-day city and has been an artery of business and trade for over a century, mainlining people, money, and commercial goods into its bloodstream. At around 300 meters wide and broader than much of the river Thames, the very use of the word "creek" is a lone beacon of modesty surviving from the city's humbler past. For when it comes to defining Dubai's modern urban environment, hyperbole, rather than understatement, is generally the order of the day.

The western shore of the Creek is referred to as Bur Dubai (a corruption of the Arabic word *bar* or place) and previously this was the heart of the city, before the New Dubai of the Sunday supplements usurped the title. Despite its waning importance, in Bur Dubai you can still find the two essential institutions that in the past constituted a proper Gulf sheikhdom: the Majlis Al Hakam (Ruler's Court) and the Masjed Al Khabeer (Grand Mosque). Here political power and religion sit side by side, though one should never forget that it is the former that exercises true control on worldly matters.

Deira, on the eastern side, is definitely the poor relation and traditionally has been home to Dubai's less-moneyed residents. Though Deira is now an integral part of the city, it did not get there by a straight path. In 1939, the ruling Maktoum family had to reaffirm their position as the undisputed rulers of Deira when a breakaway clan of the family started showing signs of sedition and seized control.

The power play that settled this dispute runs like an Arabian version of *The Godfather*'s final scene. One fine day, Sheikh Rashid (son and heir of the ruling Sheikh Said) crossed the Creek by boat (there were no bridges at this stage) to marry the daughter of a sheikh from Abu Dhabi. Sheikh Rashid had his wedding party in tow, which in this case was a bevy of armed retainers. On any other occasion, a host of sword-wielding Bedouin (*bedu* in Arabic) crossing the Creek would have been a cause for suspicion. But on his wedding day, Sheikh Rashid's entourage managed to do so without raising much concern. On arriving on the Creek's eastern shores, Sheikh Rashid's men quickly overpowered the would-be rebels and from then on, the preeminent position of the Maktoums, controlling both sides of the Creek, has never been seriously threatened.

My own arrival in Deira was much more prosaic. Dubai and I had been carrying on a long-distance relationship for some time and if a greater understanding was to be reached, a period of cohabitation was needed. The most pressing question was where to find suitable accommodation. Low-budget Deira had seemed like the best place to start, even though a former long-time resident of the city had advised against it. "You don't really want to stay there, it's a bit, you know..." he offered.

The ellipsis notwithstanding, my curiosity had been piqued. On leaving the airport, I asked my taxi driver to take me to a decent "family hotel" in Deira. In Dubai, a "clean" or family hotel means an establishment that does not double as a makeshift brothel. To find out if your hotel falls into this category, simply ask if there's a "nightclub" on the premises. If there is, asking to have your room serviced might get you more than you bargained for.

Once settled in, it was time to get acquainted with my surroundings. Despite the lateness of the hour, the urge to explore my new habitat propelled me out into the muggy night air. Bachelor residence *extraordinaire*, Deira is best known for its Arabian *souks* or markets. Yet the heart of the matter for the people who live here is Baniyas Square (also known by its original name of Nasser Square), a bustling confluence of streets and nationalities away from the spice and gold emporiums that entice tourists across the Creek to rough it with the residents for a few hours.

Dubai's global reach was evident immediately. Fur coats were advertised in shop windows with signs in the Cyrillic alphabet. Mobile phone establishments boldly declared they were "wholesale only" and the nearby pavements doubled as makeshift goods depots, as an assortment of boxes and cartons were loaded into vans and trucks. From Baniyas Square it is only a short walk to Sabkha bus station, a hustling public space where the streets teem with an assortment of nationalities. Trim Indian men wearing embroidered caps (identifying them as members of the Bohra faith, an Ismaili branch of Shia Islam) sell electronics and cheap clothing to well-fed West African women in brightly colored garments, who saunter though the crowd with bulging shopping bags balanced elegantly on their heads. Down an alleyway I came across three generations of a Chinese family manning a shop that sold (appropriately enough) china. Within 24 hours of arriving in Deira, in the course of going about my everyday business, I encountered people from Egypt, Eritrea, Cameroon, China, Nigeria, Turkmenistan, India, Pakistan, Afghanistan, Ethiopia, the Philippines, Iran, Bangladesh, and Sri Lanka. This dizzy mélange was occasionally garnished by isolated sightings of native Emiratis, looking like tourists, slightly lost. I had heard that "locals" were a minority in Dubai, but on the streets of Deira they seemed like an endangered species.

Out of all the foreigners, male members of the former Soviet Republics were the easiest to identify, given their penchant for white leather shoes, surly expressions, and the calculators hanging on cords from their necks. Throughout my stay in Deira I shared numerous hotel lifts with these ex-comrades, but not once did they greet me. Whether it is my Irish blood or excessive time spent living among salutation-conscious Arabs, I find it impossible to walk into any confined space with another human being and not at least acknowledge their presence.

This Russian reserve was in marked contrast to the young Cairenes and Alexandrians manning the *shwarma* stand close to my hotel, hawking sandwiches of coal-roasted chicken stuffed generously into pita bread. Despite the fact that Egyptians get a hard time everywhere in the Gulf (from both expatriates and locals) for being exceptional exponents of the art of palaver, there is something infectious about their upbeat approach to life, the constant joking that is the soundtrack to their daily lives, in their necessary but often unwanted Gulf exile. The little language I exchanged with the waiters standing on the streets verbally accosting the busy passing trade was highly appreciated. In fact, for the rest of my stay, each time I came within 20 meters of their patch there would be a shout in the street: "*Marhaba! Azaiyak?*" (Hello! How are you?) They would even feign annoyance when I didn't join them for a bite to eat each time I passed. Balance, it seems, is often hard to find.

By the end of that first night's walk, though now more comfortable with my physical surroundings, my metaphysical expectations of Dubai were in some disarray. I was here to paint a picture of life in this city, but the question now seemed to be *whose* life? So many nations were represented and the native one was conspicuous by its absence. To speak of a Dubai dream was a convenient generalization, but clearly there was more than one. Here were multiple narratives with little sense of demarcation. In the midst of this seething agglutination of humanity, whose experience was essential?

There was also a second source of uncertainty. Dubai was supposed to be a twenty-first-century city on the cusp of the modern world, but I was beginning to have some doubts about the extent of this much-heralded transformation. I had come here to document the brave new world emerging from the parched sands, but everything I had witnessed felt distinctly antediluvian.

Given Dubai's tiny stature and relative insignificance for all the nineteenth and most of the twentieth century, there are few stimulating portraits before its reincarnation as a regional focal point. One place where you can find fleeting descriptions is in the much-lauded travel book *Arabian Sands* by Wilfred Thesiger, an English explorer who journeyed through the deserts and mountains of the Arabian Peninsula in the late 1940s. Born in 1910 in what was then Abyssinia (Ethiopia) to a father in the employ of the British Empire, Thesiger spent his life chasing, in his own words, "savagery and beauty" across Africa, Arabia, and Asia, receiving a knighthood for his troubles. In Dubai, before heading out to explore the desert accompanied by a small band of Bedouin as guides, Thesiger strolled through the *souks* near the Creek, a place where the old ways of doing things were very much in evidence. Dubai was still only a small town of around 40,000 people and it was the lack of modern development that impressed Thesiger the most:

> The suqs *were crowded with many races – pallid Arab townsmen, armed bedu, quick-eyed and imperious; Negro slaves; Baluchis, Persians and Indians... and some Somalis off a boat from Aden. Here life moved in time with the past.*

My own first impressions were of constancy, not of change. Even if some of the players had been substituted, the game, in Deira at least, seemed to have remained the same. Though Thesiger is the gold standard by which all accounts of Arabia are measured, I had intended to distance myself from him and the other "sand-crazed Englishmen" who had written extensively about the region. After all, I wasn't in Dubai to chase shadows. From his writing, it's clear that Thesiger's obsession had been those far-removed places in the desert where the motor car and thus modernity could not follow. Anyway, the death knell for this Old Arabia had sounded years ago. Leafing through books written by men whose vision of the world had been forged by a now defunct empire had seemed like a pointless exercise. The Dubai I had in my sights was a place that had not so much embraced modernity but was actively trying to define it.

Yet each day as the newspapers trumpeted the latest statistics and proclaimed the magnificence of the Dubai dream, I found it more and more difficult to leave the past fully behind. As *Emirates News* (a saccharine, government-friendly television news show) kept pumping out the statistics each night ("Mutton Imports Up a Record God-Knows-What Percent This Year!"), I found myself retreating to descriptions of the city written thirty, forty, fifty years before, rather than the babble of newsprint that appeared outside my hotel room each day.

And Thesiger is a hard man to ignore. Every bookshop in Dubai prominently displays his works, filled with vivid descriptions and photographs of the region's Bedouin culture, recounting in detail a way of life that has disappeared for ever. For him, new ways of doing things held little appeal. He cherished the distances that existed between cultures. But the Dubai dream of the twenty-first century is all about abrading these cultural boundaries and blurring the lines that separate people from one another. Nevertheless, as I leafed through my hardback edition of *Arabian Sands*, I imagined the stern-faced gentleman in tweeds staring out from the back flap gently rebuking me for my tardiness: "You're too late, old chap. No use coming around now, you should have got here years ago!"

During my first few days in the city, I began each taxi ride by asking the same question: "What country are you from?" After a week, this changed to: "So, what part of Pakistan are you from?" And after a month: "How are things in Peshawar?" By the end it was easier just to say: "*Senga yai?*" ("How are you?" in Pashto). Peshawar is a city in the North-West Frontier Province of Pakistan close to the Afghan border and has something of a "Wild West" reputation.

Every ride was an education. I learned that when a Pakistani from the border regions near Afghanistan with little formal schooling gets fed up with the Taliban and US Special Forces fighting it out in his village and starts thinking about a move abroad, driving a taxi in Dubai is often his first port of call. For despite having a reputation for being fearsome adversaries in combat, the Pashto-speaking Pathan tribes have other talents. One of these is a natural disposition toward the automotive arts. When an Indian taxi driver in Dubai lamented that Pathans were terrible drivers, accusing them of importing driving techniques directly from the Khyber Pass, a native of Peshawar responded by insisting that timid Indian drivers were the bane of his existence, as they drove "slowly, slowly" and were always holding him up.

When it came to conversation openers with this particular demographic, it was the Irish cricket team who provided an unexpected but much-welcomed ice-breaker. Only a few weeks before, this amateur-filled team had knocked Pakistan out of the Cricket World Cup. Pakistan's ignominious defeat to Ireland was the shock of the tournament and this often led to impromptu cricketing discussions while taxiing across the city. One driver believed that the Irish had batted well, commending a solid display against England the day before, but lacked real depth in bowling. After such conversations, I mentally slapped myself on the back that my homeland, in the words of that great Irish nationalist Robert Emmet, had "taken its place among the nations of the world."

Such familiarity with my roots was in marked contrast to what I had become accustomed to in other parts of the Gulf. Conversations regarding my nationality often followed a different pattern.

"*Min wayn balad inta?*" ("What country are you from?")

"*Eir-land, Ana Eir-landi.*" ("Ireland, I am Irish.") If this makes no impression I repeat myself in English, then once more in Arabic.

"*Min Holland? Taqalam inglizi quais!*" ("From Holland? You speak English very well!") was a not atypical response.

However, after a week of dining out on Ireland's unexpected sporting success, I was brought back to earth on a trip across town. After discussing our famous win, the taxi driver asked with an uncertain expression: "Ireland, where is this, Australia, Europe?" It was then I realized why this defeat had resonated so profoundly with the Pakistani community. Losing to a second-tier cricketing nation like Bangladesh would have been one thing, but Pakistan had suffered the added shame of losing to a country that many of its citizens had never even heard of.

Aided in part by rush-hour traffic (which provided ample time for conversation), the city's Pakistani taxi drivers shed light on the symbiotic relationship between the greater Middle East's propensity to political turbulence and the rise of Dubai. One conversation was particularly enlightening. Jaffar was in his forties and came from a village outside Peshawar. He had lived in Dubai for nearly ten years. The reality of life for expatriates further down the economic ladder is not difficult to ascertain, as in Indian and Pakistani culture it is acceptable to ask perfect strangers intimate questions such as their salary details. "My friend, I work on commission. 3,000 or 3,500 dirhams, sometimes 4,000," he told me. He said that the 3,000 AED (about US$800) he earned in Dubai was much better than the US$200 he could hope to make in Pakistan.

On that kind of money, men such as Jaffar are faced with a stark choice: family or finances. Though he had wed in 2003 and had two children, he wasn't expecting to bring his wife to Dubai any time soon. When I asked if he had a room somewhere, he told me that the one-man, one-room option was simply not on the cards, given the huge surge in rent in recent years: "Not one person, one room, because it's too much expensive, so my family man, my cousin, my brother, my brother's son, eight persons take one room. 2,550 is the monthly rent, for one person coming 600–700, rent and food everything. So if a man brings his wife, total salary goes to rent."

Despite these circumstances Dubai was still an attractive proposition, especially given its relative proximity to home, to which he could return for two months once a year. "Special my area, my village, every house has one, two, three person in Dubai, because there is my friend no job," Jaffar said.

"So, maybe in Peshawar there are only women and no men – all the men in Dubai!" I chipped in, which gave him no end of amusement.

Although large numbers of these men hail from parts of the world that espouse conservative Islamic beliefs, foreigners don't have to change their habits and norms to live in Dubai. There are none of the stick-wielding religious police or *mutaween* from Saudi Arabia's Commission for the Promotion of Virtue and Prevention of Vice patrolling the streets of Satwa or Karama. And many western expatriates in Dubai live in a hermetically sealed cultural bubble and never experience the long-term daily contact with Arab culture that can lead you unconsciously to make subtle changes in your behavior. After years living in spatially conscious Gulf societies, I occasionally find myself twisting and contorting in crowded pubs in Ireland to avoid bumping into women, while I sometimes have to remember that when shaking hands with a man, you generally don't hold on to his hand for five minutes as you continue your conversation.

There is an honesty to geography that is sometimes lost with history. A city can claim to be many things, but the most straightforward way to separate facts and fictions is to go for a walk. To introduce myself properly to this new metropolis, I established a routine that consisted of a morning stroll along the Creek between 5 and 7 a.m. The timing was only partly to deal with lingering jetlag: it was also the only time cool enough to do so in comfort. In summer, the heat is a constant companion as seething daytime sun gives way each night to an even more oppressive humidity. Even in the morning there was little let-up in the muggy weather, which turned the sweaty shirts of my fellow walkers into shifting Rorschach tests with which to unravel my slowly awakening unconscious. And despite the earliness of my morning perambulations, I was rarely alone.

Although my marital status indicates otherwise, in the nomenclature of Dubai I temporarily qualified as a "bachelor," a man who had left his family behind to pursue his fortune in the city. After a few days strolling in the company of these men from both Pakistan and India, my instinct to wear shorts gave way to more restrained tracksuit bottoms, though this was only partly influenced by the stern, full-bearded man who power-walked past me, pumping his arms in the air as he went.

My decision to adopt what is known in the region as "conservative dress" was sealed by a lone western couple out for their morning jog. The joggers were clad in body-hugging spandex ensembles, while many of the walkers favored the *salwar kameez*, the long, buttock-covering shirt and baggy trousers popular in Pakistan and Afghanistan. The sight of this odd couple, particularly the woman with her midriff exposed and skintight shorts spray-painted onto her body, generated a great deal of staring among my early-morning companions. Official statistics insist that the ratio of men to women in Dubai is about 3:1, but in Deira I wouldn't be surprised if the figure is 10:1. My fellow walkers' attention may also have been arrested by the fact that it was the well-toned and sinewy female who was out ahead, setting a brisk pace while her pudgier and more flaccid male partner huffed and puffed about five yards behind her. This must have been quite a role reversal from what many of these men were accustomed to seeing back home.

My morning constitutionals also passed by the old wooden sailing ships or *dhows* that were berthed six deep at the long wharf alongside the Creek, eight-foot-high piles of cargo sitting on the docks waiting to be stevedored aboard. Here was an eclectic mix of goods bound for retail-challenged nation states. There were washing machines, fridges, and tires destined for Iran, and from what I could gather shampoo for Somalia. (Despite almost two decades of civil war and the absence of a functioning government, people still want to look good.) As I cast my gaze across the Creek to the skyscrapers of the financial district, I was reminded how Dubai is truly a twenty-first-century city. Unlike New York or London, which profess to have universal standards when it comes to business and trade, in Dubai multiple rules and regulations can exist side by side, depending on the client. Dubai can do business just as easily with a Mogadishu warlord or the London Stock Exchange.

Amidst all this cargo, which was stored out in the open overnight with little or no security, one item in particular caught my attention. A car (whose make I couldn't identify) sat on the wharf with its engine deposited alongside it. To find an answer, I introduced myself to the crew. The deckhand was a Baluchi (an ethnic group that straddles the Iran–Pakistan border), the captain an Arabic-speaking Iranian. I enquired about the ship's destination – Iran – and the car – a Paykan, an Iranian car based on a British classic, the 1960s-era Hillman Hunter. The ship was full to the brim, with cargo crammed into every available square inch. Nearby, one of the larger vessels had a truck sitting on the deck, its cabin piled high with trays of soft drinks.

All the boats berthed along Dubai's Creek plow trade routes across the Persian Gulf and the Arabian Sea that are centuries old. Nearly thirty years before, the English travel writer Jonathan Rabin had walked this same route and when I leafed through his reminiscences some time later, I was hard pressed to tell the difference between his experience and my own:

> *The dhows made up a small, self-sufficient, waterborne city in themselves... floating general stores, festooned with... Korean refrigerators, Japanese washing machines... sacks of steel wire... two dozen Taiwanese motor tires... along the wharf, other dhows were similarly weighed down.*

Though there was a certain reassurance in this continuity with the past, a scent of suspicion lingered. Had the much-heralded transformation of the city been overstated? Was the Dubai dream being touted across the globe simply a case of successful branding dreamed up by a hit squad of marketing mercenaries?

I was refining my tactics on how best to pursue my probe of the city. Some initial requests for interviews with local journalists had gone unanswered. The only person willing to comment on the Dubai dream was a British woman who no longer lived there. I had been warned in advance that only those who were paid to sing the city's praises would be keen to talk. In truth, I wasn't that disappointed: the thought of listening to a PR executive explaining the exact reasons behind the massive increase in mutton imports gave me the shivers.

So at first, I drifted. And as I wandered the streets and alleyways, the city came to me, in whatever form it so desired. It was clear that this was not simply a place with many stories to tell. The sheer range of global citizens you can find dancing at Dubai's global crossroads convinced me that a definitive understanding would be hard to pin down. There was a whole host of stories in these teeming crowds and I wanted to hear them all. And somewhere amid this broad palette of impressions and amalgam of experiences, a true portrait of the city might just reveal itself.

Nevertheless, every wanderer in new lands can benefit from a guide, and in Arabia this is particularly true. While flicking through the pages of *Arabian Sands* I discovered that even the imperious Sir Wilfred depended on a particular Arabian custom to circumvent some of the problems of unfamiliar territory. Though he had relied on Bedouin from the Al Rashid tribe to guide him on his journeys, even they had needed some outside assistance when traveling through parts of the desert traditionally controlled by a different tribe:

> *To travel safely among the Duru we needed a rabia or companion, who could frank us through their territory. He could be either from the Duru or from some other tribe entitled by tribal custom to give his travelling companions protection... while they were in his company.*

As luck would have it, when I went trawling for Dubai dreams I had a *rabia* of my own to guide me, though not necessarily one of whom Sir Wilfred would have approved.

2

Genuine Fake

"WATCHES SIR? Rolex, Breitling, Cartier, Gucci, Tag... good copy, genuine fake!" The Mumbaiker loitering on the bustling street corner didn't look like an authorized dealer for luxury brands, but I followed him all the same. We walked down a nearby alley away from the crowds and into an apartment building. Taking a lift to the second floor, he knocked on a nondescript door that opened to reveal an Aladdin's cave of fake designer handbags, watches, belts, wallets, and briefcases. The aforementioned Rolex started at 400 dirhams (about US$100) but as my interest decreased, so did the price: 350... 300... 250... 200... before he settled on 150. Though I ultimately declined to purchase, he was good natured about my refusal. And as I made my way out he welcomed me back, any time.

I was looking for Lincoln. My North American friend with a Latin American soul had recently moved to Dubai hoping to make his fortune in the city's booming import–export business, and he had offered to shine a light into some of the less well-publicized nooks and crannies. After fifteen years bouncing around the various petro-sheikhdoms of the Gulf, Lincoln was looking to make it big in Dubai.

But in the back streets of Deira, fake designer goods are not the only contraband on offer. An unctuous little man with pointed disco-era shirt collars approached me with a crawling smile: "You want lady? India, Russia, China, what you like? Only hundred dirhams! And ten for me, commission!" In parts of Dubai, a fake Rolex costs more than a real human being.

Cities in the Gulf only come alive at night. Though it was well after midnight, the streets were still full of people who clearly had little intention of retiring to bed any time soon. While my early-morning walks were pleasant, the searing hot afternoons were better suited to siestas, girding oneself for when the sun went down. Down another alley-way in front of a small hotel, two Pakistani men were sweating profusely in the humid night air as they packed wooden containers with an assortment of goods for ship-ment overseas. Inside, the lobby was a hive of activity. A gaggle of *babushkas* were chattering away, reincarnated as impromptu businesswomen on their way home to Azerbaijan with large bags crammed with sandals and clothes. At the doorway, an officious-looking man stood with a clipboard beside an industrial weighing scale. This hotel also doubled as the local air-freight headquarters of an Azeri air carrier bound for Baku.

Given such surroundings, you could only admire the optimism of the nearby Yaoundé Palace hotel. The brass plaque mounted outside the entrance was adorned with a single lonely star. I imagined a slow process of refurbish-ments and upgrades (the addition of a toilet seat perhaps), each milestone marked by the manager bringing out a mal-let and chisel to carve out another star. On entering the lobby, the receptionist looked at me with a mixture of bemusement and suspicion, but I just pointed upward. Lincoln had telephoned to say he would be spending the evening in the restaurant upstairs.

After midnight, it seemed that the "restaurant" also doubled as a flop house for a host of young West African men whose Dubai dream was temporarily on hold. (Describing them as customers would be inaccurate – surely money has to change hands?) Some were sitting with their heads resting on the plastic tables, others were laid back on the old battered sofas, fast asleep. Here I found Lincoln, sitting with the owner, shooting the breeze and dreaming big.

Over dinner, which consisted of an array of Cameroonian stews, Lincoln told me about his own business plans, while also shedding light on Dubai's import-export business and the emirate's expanding African connection: "They re-export everything here. Containers are shipped from China in bulk, they only sell in big quantities, maybe an entire container of oil filters. After the different containers come to Dubai, the Africans come along and buy the different spare parts they need and consolidate it all in one container. Then they ship it back to Africa. Did you know that Dubai is the world's second largest exporter of spare parts?"

There were many things I didn't know. But at least by the end of the evening, some of the gaps in my knowledge had been filled. I now understood why the shops in the nearby Gold Souk were looking to buy uncut diamonds. Even the "wholesale only" signs in Baniyas Square began to make sense: these shops were only interested in bulk sales. In fact, the mobile phone business between Dubai and Cameroon was so buoyant that a suburb of the Cameroonian city of Akwa had even acquired the name "Dubai." However, going from one Cameroonian journalist's report, this African suburb thousands of miles away wasn't attracting the most upstanding citizens of the nation: "The town harbours all the bad boys, all the bad places and so on. It is a town where people hustle to make ends meet." After trying their hand back home, the next step for many of these "bad boys" was to move to the real Dubai and continue this tradition of hustling to survive – with varying degrees of success. (Months later, I learned from Lincoln that the "bad boy" of that night's group turned out to be the restaurant manager himself, who was now helping the police with their enquiries regarding some counterfeit US currency.)

As we talked into the night, Lincoln regaled me with stories from his time on the Gringo Trail through South America, decades before. He insisted that travelers had it easy nowadays. Back then, his only source of illumination had been a tome called the *South American Handbook*.

Looking around the room, I was glad that my time in Dubai had coincided with Lincoln's. I could have walked the streets for months and never come across this place. And there's always a certain satisfaction when the manager comes out from the behind the counter and pulls up a chair. With Lincoln's help, the anonymous faces on every street were beginning to take on some definition. I now felt I was on the inside looking out rather than the other way around. When it came to exploring Dubai's African under-belly (up until that night I didn't even know it had one), Lincoln had proven to be a perfect *rabia*. When I told him about my early-morning walks along the Creek and the eclectic mounds of cargo, Lincoln immediately had an idea, an entranceway to another of Dubai's multifarious communities.

"You need to meet my friend Ahmad," he said. "He's a crazy Iranian guy, you'll like him."

A few days later, we called on Ahmad. His office was located in the mazy spare parts *souk* behind Baniyas Square, a warren of narrow streets where Baluchi, Pakistani, and Afghani men pushed flat trolleys and wheel-barrows laden with an assortment of motor parts. They are just one tiny link in a global supply chain that can stretch from a factory in southern China to a mechanic's workshop in the Nigerian interior. As we climbed the stairs, Lincoln described a wrestling match he had witnessed downstairs between two Chinese men and a Nigerian over some business deal that had gone wrong. The Indian security guard had locked the three of them inside the lobby and called the police to sort it out – just a little kink in the global economy at work.

Ahmad was born in western Iran, but Dubai was now his home, just as it is for hundreds of thousands of his fellow countrymen. Since the overthrow of the Shah in 1979 and the establishment of the Islamic Republic of Iran, Dubai has served as an outlet valve for that country's pent-up desires and dreams. Iranian singers who must perform secretly at home can do so openly here. And for many young men and women from Shiraz or Esfahan, the first time they dance to Iranian music in an Iranian nightclub without fear of censure will be across the Gulf in Dubai. But along with such distractions, Iranian entrepreneurs also come to do business beyond Tehran's centrally planned and crony-filled economy.

Though taking a phone call from a supplier, Ahmad beckoned us inside. His business model, on the surface at least, was simple. Ahmad imported spare parts from France into Dubai and then facilitated their re-export to Iran. Why the French company involved couldn't just export this stuff directly to Iran is the billion-dirham question to which Dubai prays its regional neighbors never find the answer. Be it international sanctions, bureaucracy, inefficiency, corruption, or logistical problems (or more likely a combination of all of these), there is an absence of confidence among the global business community when it comes to doing business with Iran. The people talking to Ahmad believed they could do business through Dubai, although this confidence is not a recent phenomenon, as the city has been an epicenter of assurance for quite some time.

It all began in 1902, when the Shah of Iran imposed high customs duties on goods passing in and out of Iranian ports on the Persian Gulf. At the time, these were important transit points on a trade route that stretched from India to Europe. As a result of these taxes, goods that used to be shipped via Iran began to be moved through Dubai instead. The need to raise taxes was linked to the heavy spending habits of the reigning monarch in Iran; Dubai is ever ready to profit from the short-sightedness and strategic ineptitude of its neighbors. The imposition of duties upset many Iranian merchants based in port towns all along the southern coast of Iran, some of whom were ethnic Arabs, not Persians. As a result, many set up temporary homes in Dubai to monitor the shift in their business.

By the 1920s, when it became clear that these financial impediments were here to stay, a mini-exodus occurred. Tradesmen, pearl divers, and numerous other workers associated with the merchants' sea-faring business called time on Persia and moved permanently to Dubai. These émigrés established an Iranian quarter on the western shore of the Creek that to this day is named Bastakiyah, after the area in Iran from which many of them originally came. The houses these economic migrants built incorporated the wind towers that adorned their homes in Iran. These towers funnel breezes through specially designed chimneys into a central room beneath, providing some relief from the intense summer heat. Over time, this early form of Iranian air-conditioning has become a symbol synonymous with Dubai.

To this day, the connection between Dubai and its larger neighbor across the water is intricate and involved.

Apart from the hundreds of thousands of Iranians in the city, nearly half of all locals in Dubai are *ajam* (an Arabic term for people of Persian origin), who trace their lineage back across the Gulf to Iran. Whether you prefer the adjective Arabian or Persian depends on your nationality and/or political persuasion. Iranians use the Persian Gulf while Arabs (naturally enough) prefer the term Arabian Gulf. Traditionally, this body of water was always known as the Persian Gulf and it was only after the Pan-Arab nationalist movement took hold in the 1950s that Arabian Gulf came into fashion. (American journalists use the term Persian Gulf while their British colleagues diplomatically refer to "The Gulf"; I prefer to use all three terms interchangeably and with abandon, as one may as well embrace the confusion.) To add to the sense of uncertainty, The Gulf is sometimes used to refer to the region itself; that is, the Arab Gulf states that share a coastline with the aforementioned body of water, with the exception of Iraq and Iran.

Ajam (ayam is the Gulf pronunciation) literally means "illiterate" or "one who mumbles." This term dates back hundreds if not thousands of years to when few foreigners visited Arabia. Contact with the outside world was primarily with Persians. Over time, *ajam* acquired several meanings, such as "foreigner" or "non-Arab." Though the *ajam* of Dubai are full citizens, in the past there were disputes with ethnic overtones. To this day, some locals who have Bedouin roots from the Arabian Peninsula maintain that they are "pure" Arabs and refuse intermarriage with their fellow citizens of Iranian heritage.

This demographic shift from the Iranian coast to Dubai didn't happen by accident. This influx of restless Iranian merchants occurred during the rule of Sheikh Said (the grandfather of the current ruler), who displayed remarkable prospicience by actively encouraging the inward migration. And this move is critical in understanding the mindset that has been present in Dubai for some time. Though cynics would argue that the emirate needed all the help it could get, the belief that immigrants can ultimately be a net benefit to one's society (rather than a threat) is revolutionary thinking in many parts of the world even today, never mind a century ago.

Sheikh Said's son, Sheikh Rashid, continued the city's tradition of being a business-friendly environment. "What's good for the merchants is good for Dubai" is the adage most attributed to this former ruler. Though relatively prosperous in the 1950s, Dubai was certainly not an economic powerhouse. It was around this time that Sheikh Rashid sold a number of bonds to finance the dredging and expansion of the Creek in order to accommodate more commercial shipping. This proved a success. His next project was considerably more ambitious. In the 1970s, the largest manmade port in the world was built in Jebel Ali, which was followed by a Free Trade Zone in the 1980s. At the time this was seen as a foolish enterprise, and pessimists joked about a massive white elephant standing empty in the desert.

The next generation of the Maktoum family continued this expansion and began to look beyond the region. Sheikh Rashid was succeeded by his son (the late Sheikh Maktoum who ruled from 1990 to 2006) and then by another son, the current ruler Sheikh Mohammed. It was during this time that Asian economies such as China and India, who were once incapable of even feeding themselves, exploded into life. Dubai became the key transit point for a new global economy desperately in need of a link between East and West, just like those sailing ships that needed a home over a century ago. Dubai became a major hub for global trade and as the travelers, businessmen, cargo ships, airplanes, and money passed through, the cash register of Dubai Inc. rang with the sweet sound of yet another sale.

Apart from his being an ebullient host, the time spent in Ahmad's office was also a lesson in efficiency. When the heat of the day became too much, I could just sit there over coffee and Iranian sweets and let Dubai come to me. For Ahmad's world was a miniature of Dubai itself: a nexus between two worlds, a place where the producers of the East can interface with the consumers of the West, and vice versa when the need arises. While multibillion-dollar takeover deals are planned in Dubai, you can also find people doing business in ways that have not changed in centuries. By using the trust that can only come from familial bonds, businessmen like Ahmad overcome the biggest impediment in the global marketplace: fear of the unknown. Other Iranians in the same trade would pop in for a chat or an Indian sales rep from HSBC would walk from office to office, offering much-needed overdrafts. Though Ahmad was interested, much of his operation was still done the old way. Some payments from Iran came through the *hawala* system of unofficial cash transfers, unregulated and undocumented, which has been operating in the region for many years.

Since the 1979 revolution, Iran's somewhat idiosyncratic approach to international diplomacy has isolated it from much of the global economy. The resulting uncertainty, combined with the sheer unpredictability of the political situation in Tehran, has led to a massive influx of Iranians into Dubai, which has become a vital import and export hub for the Iranian economy. And along with the white economy, if there are sanctions to be busted or embargoes circumvented, this is when Dubai's Iranian community steps in. It's not only spare parts for Citroëns and Peugeots that pass through the city en route to Iran. When the Iranian government is looking to buy spare parts for its aging fleet of American military aircraft (during the Shah's time the US and Iran were on much friendlier terms), Iranian businessmen in Dubai are often the middlemen, even though the US has placed sanctions on such sales. There have even been reports that Iran (with the help of Pakistan) has sought to build the Big One through Dubai.

As such, the newspapers sometimes carried reports of visiting American officials encouraging the stronger enforcement of economic sanctions against Iran. Given the see-sawing tensions and the insincere veneers of diplomacy between the US and Iran, the genuine good cheer between Ahmad and Lincoln was an uplifting lesson in Persian–American relations. Here was a space where people could ignore the malfeasance and rhetoric of their governments, in keeping with Dubai's image as a place where Middle Eastern swords get tempered into plowshares; somewhere where concord, rather than conflict, is given a chance to take flight.

3
Maktoum Inc.

AS THE HORSES SPED AROUND THE FINAL TURN, I leaned over the rails to catch a glimpse of the most pampered animals on the planet thundering down the home straight. All around me, a bustling crowd of Westerners, dressed in their best faux-Ascot chic, shouted encouragement at the field as it approached the finishing line. Up in the grandstand, a large concentration of locals in pristine white robes were watching the action in a more detached fashion. Although the Nad Al Sheba racetrack is just a short hop from the city, tonight it felt as far as from Deira as Doncaster. This was most definitely a change of scene.

"It gives us great pleasure to welcome you to Nad Al Sheba racecourse for the 12th running of the Dubai World Cup." The introduction in my official program welcoming racegoers was signed by the man himself: His Highness, Sheikh Mohammed Bin Rashid Al Maktoum, Prime Minister and Vice-President of the UAE and Ruler of Dubai. Good things always come in threes. Sheikh Mohammed is respectively the brother, son, and grandson of the last three rulers of Dubai and is the tenth emir of the Al-Maktoum dynasty.

Of the three titles he enjoys, Vice-President and Prime Minister of the UAE are the equivalent of nonexecutive directorships and occupy some but not all of his attention. Much of the day-to-day running of the UAE is left to the Al Nahyans of Abu Dhabi. It is being *al Hakam* (the Ruler) of Dubai that is Sheikh Mohammed's real job. If you consult an Arabic dictionary, you will find that *al Hakam* has multiple interpretations and can also mean adjusting, adjudicating, arbitrager, arbitrating, arbiter, epigrams, fore-judging, governorship, governance, governing, judging, judgment, lording, prejudging, referee, reigning, sentencing, umpire, and wisdoms. On reflection, all of the above qualities and roles are often bundled into the job description of a Gulf ruler.

As the Ruler of Dubai, Sheikh Mohammed exercises absolute power in the emirate, answerable to no one but himself. By extension, the inner circle of the Maktoum family is where all political power lies. This is the norm not the exception in the six other emirates within the UAE as well as the other sheikhdoms along the shores of the Arabian Gulf. Despite enjoying similar degrees of absolute power, none of the ruling families in Bahrain, Oman, Kuwait, Qatar, or Saudi Arabia has earned such a close association with business dynamism. Though the city acquired the unofficial title of Dubai Inc. due to its pro-business stance, Maktoum Inc. may be a more appropriate tag given the level of control the ruling family exerts on the business environment, both overtly and covertly.

Taking a corporate approach to government, Sheikh Mohammed is both absolute monarch and CEO, though his benign dictatorship is certainly more Silicon Valley than Saddam Hussein. Unlike the secular dictatorships of Egypt and Syria, which prefer to control their populations with a stick, the rulers of the Gulf states have always preferred to proffer carrots. While ordinary "locals" (the term by which citizens of Dubai and the other Emirates are referred to) have no political power or any influence over important decisions, there is an unofficial "ruling bargain" at work that is certainly not a master/slave relationship. The locals accept that *al Hakam* holds absolute authority, but there is an understanding that he must provide for all of his people (expatriates are expected to take care of themselves). As a result, locals are entitled to free housing, education, healthcare, and more or less guaranteed employment. In this regard, Dubai is a twenty-first-century entity built on ancient Bedouin principles. Lucre begets loyalty and vice versa.

When it comes to affairs of state, Sheikh Mohammed is known to prefer the company of business leaders and entrepreneurs to diplomats and government officials. His leadership style is also defined by a certain distance from geopolitical affairs. Dubai seems to have realized long ago that there is no profit in Middle East politics; you never see Sheikh Mohammed at regional summits trying to get the Palestinians and the Israelis to kiss and make up. Business initiatives and depoliticized charitable foundations are more his style, but horse racing is his passion.

Styling itself as the highlight of the world's flat racing season, the Dubai World Cup is but one of many international sporting events that Dubai has used to market itself as both the region's premier playground and a global tourist destination. While the Epsom Derby boasts a more ancient pedigree and its counterpart across the pond in Kentucky packs in bigger crowds, Dubai has taken a straightforward approach to its lack of history and sporting kudos – money. By upping the prize money to US$6 million for the feature race, the organizers have simply outbid the competition. But the Dubai World Cup is as much a personal indulgence as an expression of the emirate's global business ambitions. It is a hobby underwritten by a considerable budget – Sheikh Mohammed is a billionaire many times over and the Maktoum clan's love affair with thoroughbred race horses has seen them spend over a billion dollars on bloodstock over the years. Sheikh Mohammed even underwrites the costs incurred by other owners in getting their horses and people to Dubai to compete.

The queue to gain entry to the racecourse the day of the big race was a multicultural paradise of people from across the globe. Once inside, however, the sense of unity quickly dissolved. Westerners headed to the Irish pubs, Arabs sat down at a *shisha* café, while an array of Africans, Indians, and Pakistanis brought out picnics and ensconced themselves under the shade of whatever trees were available. Sitting on the grass with the latter group, I engaged in some people-watching using for reference a local tabloid, which lampooned the different punters one might expect to see at today's event. An aging Hooray Henry was easily identifiable, strutting around like a peacock in a luminous suit trying to attract the attention of a leather-skinned bleached-blonde lady of leisure nearby. Consulting the paper again, I identified this female variety as a Jumeirah Jane.

It was members of this latter group who held the attention of the young Sudanese and Yemeni men seated on the grass beside me. Dressed in baseball caps, baggy jeans, and basketball shirts, they looked out of place among the red-faced and sun-tinged Anglo-Saxons who dominated the crowd. I fell into conversation with Omar, a young man studying music production whose parents had lived here for years. He gave me the lowdown on college life in the city.

"Dubai, it's like New York," he said.

"Like New York?" I was more than a little skeptical. Did Dubai really have an alternative music scene of the kind that sets London and New York apart from mere pretenders? To my mind, if Dubai were to be personified by a musical Welshman it would have to be a sing-along Tom Jones rather than an avant-garde John Cale.

"Well, not really, we don't have many places to go," Omar added. It was also clear that it wasn't the horses that had brought him and his friends here for the day. Surveying the crowd, Omar remarked wistfully in his best G-funk drawl, "All these beautiful white ladies and I can't get some!" Now, while the second adjective may have been correct, the preceding one was open to some debate. Dubai (like many other countries in the Middle East) can be an attractive place for Caucasian women to live if they are desirous of male company. For as long as they have blonde hair and white skin, they need never want for companionship. In fact, there is a particular phenomenon whereby some expatriate women become progressively blonder the longer they remain in the region.

Returning to my tabloid, I checked out the odds for the big race, which were clearly printed in the paper even though gambling is prohibited in Dubai. Instead of the Tote, there was a free Pick 7 lottery, offering prizes if you could guess the winners of all seven races. A long-term Dubai expat told me that previously, corporate sponsors had found a way around the prohibition through an intricate system of tickets and prizes. You simply bought a number of "tickets" for the horse that you wanted to back. If your nag won, you received a prize corresponding to the number of tickets you bought. My confidant explained with a wink, "There was always someone on hand to 'buy' the prizes off you there and then."

Under the Maktoums, Dubai has become adept at pursuing multiple approaches to development. Traditional interpretations of Islam are still the norm for the local population, while foreigners are generally allowed all the creature comforts they need. Thus gambling (for the time being at least) is deemed an undesirable vice, whereas alcohol is legal, despite the fact that the ban on gambling appears in the same verses of the Quran where both are deemed *haram* (forbidden):

They ask you (O Muhammad Peace Be Upon Him) concerning alcoholic drink and gambling. Say: "In them is a great sin, and (some) benefit for men, but the sin of them is greater than their benefit."

Satan wants only to excite enmity and hatred between you with intoxicants (alcoholic drinks) and gambling, and hinder you from the remembrance of Allah and from As-Salat (the prayer). So, will you not then abstain?

The reason Dubai draws a distinction between alcohol and gambling could develop into an analysis of differing schools of Islamic jurisprudence, but there is a simpler explanation. The Maktoums have always been aware of the needs of the foreigners Dubai requires to propel its economy forward. Saudi Arabia, with its vast reserves of oil, can afford to be prohibitive. In any case, while the proposed 15 million tourists a year that Dubai envisions as the future of the city may not mind gambling restrictions, taking away their beer and wine (and the massive revenue they generate) is another proposition altogether. It seems that in this case the benefit of alcohol outweighs the harm. A closer examination of the Quranic text also reveals that the believer is asked to "abstain" not "prohibit" the demon drink, as is the case in more conservative Islamic states. Anyway, while the Dubai ruling family strongly embraces local traditions, it is not so concerned with prohibitions. The government of Dubai owned a major shareholding in MGM Mirage, the world's largest gambling company. Thus it can be argued that some of the money that pays for Dubai's roads, hospitals, and even its mosques has come from gaming.

In any case, modern technology can make nonsense of prohibition. On the day I attended the racing tipsters were insisting that the main event was literally a two-horse race, between Discreet Cat, owned by Sheikh Mohammed's Godolphin stable, and an American "raider" trained in Tennessee by the name of Invasor. I was going for the latter. My selection had been simplified by a fortuitous encounter in the airport duty-free shop the night before. In the midst of a dizzying selection of Burgundy and Zinfandel, a face familiar from television emerged from behind the cigars. It belonged to Derek Thompson, a horse-racing presenter on British television. It didn't take a detective to figure out what he was in town for. Despite being cornered for the inside scoop on the following day, he was very good natured about the intervention. And when I asked for a tip, he gave me some abstemious advice a Grand Mufti would be proud of: "Keep your hands in your pockets... but Invasor will win." All it took was a text message to a friend in Ireland who has a penchant for internet gambling and within minutes a reply came through: "Invasor: 10 bucks at 11/8 to win. Good luck!" My throwaway wager wasn't going to pay for a night in the Burj Al Arab Hotel, but at least I now had a vested interest in the result of the big race.

Up in the main grandstand, Sheikh Mo (as Dubai's Ruler and self-styled CEO is known) was resplendent in a gold *kandura*, the traditional robe worn by men in the Gulf region. The feature race was due to start once the obligatory opening ceremony had been unleashed on the crowd now gathered around the paddock. I was receiving a running commentary on the proceedings from a mini headphone-radio set, distributed free of charge to all the punters. This was tuned to an FM radio station providing live coverage of the race meeting – the kind of customer-oriented approach that Dubai excels at and that sets it apart from its neighbors. The disembodied voices of two English radio DJs were promising something "very special" once the opening ceremony got underway.

Apart from a sense of anticipation over the opening ceremony, they were extremely excited over recently revealed plans for a development called Meydan, which was very much Sheikh Mohammed's pet project. This was a new "Horse City" to replace the existing Nad al Sheba racetrack, which I must admit looked perfectly fine to me. The plan was simple: the existing grandstand was to be razed to the ground and a new one built in its place. This major project was scheduled to be completed in only a couple of years. One presumes there were no problems getting planning permission. A similar quick-fire approach was taken when it became clear that the city was growing faster than its transport capabilities and needed a metro. In the rest of the Arab world it would have taken years of arguing just to get a toy train set up and running. In Dubai, planning had been much simpler and a rapid transit system was built in a couple of years. This was the route the metro was to follow and that was it, any complaints to be forwarded to His Highness.

Through all this chatter in my ear there was one recurring motif: Sheikh Mohammed's overall magnificence. The Gulf can be a difficult place for a republican, as the fawning platitudes commentators use to describe the hereditary monarchies are very hard to digest. Even though Sheikh Mohammed himself insists that Brand Dubai is not a one-man show, this doesn't stop the local media metaphorically wetting themselves in ebullience whenever they mention his name. The comparisons are usually somewhere between a modern-day Haroun Al Rashid and Lorenzo de' Medici, cooking up an Arab renaissance-cum-rebirth on the shores of the Gulf while turning Dubai into a futurist Florence. Even the architects of the Palm projects used the artificial islands to spell out one of Sheikh Mohammed's epigrams in Arabic script. While such obsequiousness is not uncommon in the region, it was disagreeable to find English voices offering up the sycophancy one regularly hears in the Arab media. Surely one can protest too much?

Though the moneymen behind Maktoum Inc. tout the city as a bastion of economic opportunity, the dividing line between what is government owned and Maktoum owned is opaque. The Dubai dream is controlled by a complex web of holding companies. The multilimbed Dubai Holding is owned by the Dubai Government, but Sheikh Mohammed (as the Ruler of Dubai) owns 99 percent of the shares. (The figure is actually 99.67 percent; I wondered who owned the other 0.33 percent.) Even "private" companies such as Emaar and Nakeel behind the mega-projects like Burj Dubai, Dubailand, and The Palm Jumeirah are part owned by the Dubai Government and are only partially listed on the Dubai stock exchange. On top of this, these are nowhere near normal commercial operations; for example, Emaar gets the land it builds on in Dubai "free" from the government (that is, Sheikh Mohammed). In the past, there have been rumors of jiggery-pokery by the big players (which by definition includes the ruling family and/or people very close to them) at the expense of ordinary shareholders.

Thus, despite the claims of many eager commentators, Dubai is not a city built by capitalism. It has been built by capital, but without the constrictive tail of an -ism. Dubai practices *à la carte* capitalism, giving the market free rein so long as there is some benefit in doing so. Though most major projects are carried out by organizations that may appear and act like private companies, a closer look reveals something different. All major concerns are ultimately controlled by the ruling élite of the Maktoums, who can cherry-pick which of Milton Friedman's guiding principles suit them best. Despite the lack of transparency, both local and foreign financiers insist that Dubai's economic transformation could not have occurred without a revolution in the crippling bureaucracy and restrictive business practices that are still common practice among its neighbors.

A local financier once explained the Dubai business model to me in the following terms: "They have basically turned government departments into private companies and have them competing against each other. In other Gulf countries, these guys would be government ministers, but here they are CEOs, that's why things get done so quickly, even though there must be a huge conflict of interest." He also explained that the same people sit on the boards of "private" companies and "government" bodies such as Dubai's Executive Council; inverted commas are often required when discussing this unique approach to governance and public policy. Though overall, the financier believed that the model works. "There is always a conflict of interest everywhere between politics and business," he said, dissecting the symbiotic relationship that exists between the US and British Governments and large defense contractors such as Halliburton and BAE. He added, "But when you line up the positives against the negatives in Dubai, there is no doubt that the good stuff outweighs the bad."

As the evening progressed, the energetic English voices in my ear began to feel like a Dubai conscience: any time a negative notion sprang to mind, it was swatted away by the thought police unabashedly singing the praises of the emirate. They were now waxing lyrical about the opening ceremony, which was just about to start. The theme of the performance was the taming of the wild Arabian horse. To this effect, the lights around the stadium were dimmed and loud music struck up around the racetrack. A film depicting the domestication of the Arabian horse was shown across a huge screen mounted along the finish line. The extravaganza began with footage of Arabian horses running wild in the desert before being captured and tamed. As the film projected these images into the night, fireworks crackled in the darkness and horsy acrobatics and pyrotechnics were on display in the paddock. The finale involved men levitating in the air behind the screen and a cavalry in *kanduras* galloping down the home straight – an Arabian-themed charge of the light brigade.

I was impressed. The only thing that troubled me was the fate of the Arabian horse. Once wild, untamed, and free, these magnificent beasts were now destined to be pampered and fretted over, forever to be primped and preened in a gilded captivity. This struck me as a possible metaphor for the progress Dubai itself has experienced. Not long ago this had been a frontier town, a place where the Bedouin of the desert rubbed shoulders with seafarers and adventurers, where explorers like Thesiger sojourned before departing for the wild Arabian sands. Had Dubai's recent thrust for modernization broken the spirit of a once exciting frontier town? Or were people who yearned for past times simply unreconstructed sentimentalists with nothing better to do than gripe about the ineluctable progress of time? After all, the horses looked happy enough, despite the fact they had been broken.

By the time the big race finally got underway later that evening, I had taken up a position against the railings along the finishing straight. A silence descended on the crowd as the starter marshaled the field. After taking a moment to settle, the horses burst out from the starting gates. Invasor (my selection) made the running from the start, while Sheikh Mohammed's Discreet Cat hung back near the rear. By the time the field reached the final turn, Discreet Cat had tailed off completely. After a tight contest to the finishing line, Invasor beat off a Saudi-owned horse to win by 1¾ lengths, covering the 2,000 meters in just over two minutes. As the winning horse and jockey made their way to the winner's enclosure, a loud cheer went up. Clearly I wasn't the only one to have figured out a way to have a wager.

The new world champion was led by a woman, who I assumed was an American from the US-based training stable. As the colt triumphantly entered the paddock, a young man in Emirati robes took the reins to lead the horse on the victory parade. Yet even after this handover, the woman never left the side of the Emirati and continued to issue instructions (whether these were directed at the horse or the new handler I couldn't tell) as Invasor was displayed to the cheering crowd. This was a good illustration of the fact that although much of the expertise on which Dubai's success is built comes from overseas, an Emirati face must front all of its major accomplishments.

My initial impression that the US-trained Invasor was an American "raider," in town to deprive Sheikh Mohammed's Godolphin stable of victory, turned out not to be a wholly accurate depiction of events. Closer examination of the race card revealed that though Invasor was trained in the US, the horse was in fact owned by Sheikh Hamdan Bin Rashid Al Maktoum, a brother of Sheikh Mohammed.

And the question of ownership was not the only incongruity. For a race with such a grand title, I was surprised that so small a field had gone to post. This shortage of top horses was credited to a clash with the European racing calendar and a feud between Sheikh Mohammed's stable and an Irishman named John Magnier, whose Coolmore racing empire battles Godolphin at bloodstock auctions for the best horses in the world. Out of six horses, the favorite and second favorite had belonged to the Ruler of Dubai and his brother, while another contender had represented the Saudi royal family. The three other horses were fairly lightweight.

This was an elephant in the middle of the room that none of the commentators had mentioned, a specter that lingered in the shadows. Despite its ambitions, the self-styled world cup of horse racing (for the moment at least) could also be seen as just a plaything for the Maktoums. While the royal colors are seen astride mounts at Ascot, it would be very odd if the only horses with a chance of winning the 2,000 Guineas belonged to Elizabeth II, her daughter Princess Anne, or Juan Carlos I of Spain, a direct descendant of Queen Victoria.

Despite the limitations of the field, as I made my way home from the race course that evening I felt I had learned a valuable lesson. Whatever contest you find yourself involved in in Dubai, there is a very strong chance that the Maktoums are going to win.

4
Hail Britannia

We can, if we wish, make ourselves extremely unpleasant to the Trucial Sheikhs and their subjects; indeed, by cutting off supplies and the seizure of pearling dhows we can kill all these small principalities, but by proceeding to extremes we certainly run a risk of antagonising world opinion, which appears to be on the look-out for any stick which is offered for beating the British empire with.

Political Resident (1929)

THE HISTORY BETWEEN DUBAI AND BRITAIN, unlike the waters of the Gulf that brought them together, is deep. Although successive rulers from the Maktoum family have charted their own course toward development, at every stage there have been Britons at the helm providing guidance in some form or other. In the past, the English in Dubai were a small, élite band of diplomats and military personnel. They generally came to the region steeped in the culture of diplomacy, and often exquisitely versed in the manners and customs of Arabia. But today, you can also find English people working below decks. Over 100,000 Britons live in Dubai, more than the estimated 80,000 locals within the emirate. This new generation of expat English are a world away from the influential coteries of Britishers who went before them. And as they pull pints, cut hair, work in the media and advertising, and sell houses across the city, it is no surprise that the star has waned somewhat on the imperious reputation enjoyed by Her Majesty's citizens in the most dynamic of her former protectorates.

I had first come across the latest batch of British expats in all their glory on the night of the Dubai World Cup, while waiting in a seemingly endless queue for a taxi back to my hotel. After over two hours of queuing, tempers became frayed. An Englishman and his girlfriend behind me were having a full-on argument amid a group of friends. "I'll never marry her," the man slurred to his companions after receiving a verbal broadside from his beloved over some perceived slight. But his partner didn't back down. "Do you know what this guy was before I brought him here?" she fought back. "A drug addict. He was addicted to crack cocaine before we came to Dubai."

Even though I could appreciate the couple's honesty, I wondered what the local population made of them and the tens of thousands of other British expatriates now living in their home town, ever so willing to spill both their hearts and their drinks in public. And while all this banter may have been a normal night's fun back home, I could only imagine what a man like Thesiger would have made of this crowd, more Aintree than Ascot. During his time exploring the region, Sir Wilfred obviously made a rather good impression on the locals. In *Arabian Sands*, he recounts dining with the Sheikh of Dubai and spending a month or so hunting in the desert with Sheikh Zayed, the future ruler of Abu Dhabi.

It was a different British couple (getting on considerably better than these two) who came to embody this new generation of expats, which has been somewhat harshly dubbed "The Degenerates of Dubai" in the British tabloid press. That headline resulted from an infamous case when a man and woman were charged and convicted of having sex on the beach (not the cocktail) in the expatriate hangout of Jumeirah. The British pair received three months' imprisonment (the sentence was later suspended) and were expelled from the country. Though the conviction stood, the accused insisted that they were only kissing and that the charges had been exaggerated by the arresting officer, who in turn claimed that the woman had been abusive. The incident occurred after the pair had indulged in a particular Dubai custom, the drunken Friday brunch. After a long working week, these all-you-can-eat-and-drink blowouts at the city's five-star hotels get turned into a night out, but during daylight hours. Such indulgence is in marked contrast to the traditional Friday lunches enjoyed by locals. After midday prayers (the equivalent of Sunday mass), extended families in Dubai often gather in a grandparent's house for a meal, the social glue that binds much of Emirati society together.

One of the more surprising elements of this case was the lack of sympathy the couple received from many other expatriates, in no doubt partly influenced by a feeling of social superiority. A degree of snobbery has always existed among Dubai's British residents, long before the city's most recent incarnation as a dynamic global force. And it has always been a favored pastime of some to denigrate the social standing of their fellow exiles, even if this usually tells you more about the critic than the recipient.

Nevertheless, despite the demographic transformation of the last few decades, the city still holds a certain intangible appeal for Britons with itchy feet. While the opportunities for adventure and exploration that pushed men like Thesiger to Arabia all those years ago may have disappeared, there remain other factors that continue to draw people here. There is still a chance to start afresh, an opportunity for reinvention, to leave your old self behind, to get that second chance and walk through doors that are invariably shut in your face back home.

Once the reformed drug user and his girlfriend had kissed and made up, it was time for another conflagration.

Obviously annoyed at the long wait, a burly red-faced man with a shaved head jumped the queue and hopped into one of the arriving taxis. The patience of the crowd, which had been fairly well behaved until that point, finally snapped and a cacophony of angry English voices shouted at the Indian and Arab marshals to stop the taxi and eject the occupant. The red face emerged appearing somewhat distraught and appealed to the crowd. "Are any of you British? Are any of you British? I'm a staff sergeant in the Royal Marines and I have to get back to my ship. Don't you know that Iran has captured some British marines? I have to get back to my ship!" British marines patrolling the Shatt al-Arab waterway between Iraq and Iran had been picked up by the Iranians and accused of violating Iranian territorial waters.

Yet in response to the man's request, a chorus of abuse came back from the crowd: "Give him a taxi, he's off to invade Iran!" and "You're too fat to be a marine!"

Sir Wilfred, one felt, wouldn't have been amused.

Although there have been changes in personnel among the British expat population in recent years, places continue to exist where you can catch passing glimpses of the old ways. The Dubai Country Club is one such throwback to older times and is an embodiment of a more genteel expression of expatriate life. This was a place where men showed a stiff upper lip and made the best of a difficult situation. On the Al Awir desert golf course, a recreational inversion takes place. Greens become "browns" and instead of water and careful grooming, a mixture of sand and diesel is compacted to produce a smooth putting surface. In the days before mass desalination, a piece of artificial grass was all there was to compensate for the absence of any greenery on the fairway. After each shot, the ball is placed on a square of fake turf before the next stroke is played across a designated patch of desert. Such diversions were an attempt to re-create a life left behind in Britain, withering summer heat notwithstanding. For the western expatriates who came to the burgeoning oil economies of the Gulf, generous tax-free salaries usually compensated for any lifestyle compromises they had to make. However, just like the artificial grass they carried around to play golf, there was always an element of make-believe to the new lives they created for themselves.

But new ways of doing things are continually encroaching on the old. The high-end tourists that Dubai needs demand the real thing and nowadays celebrity-endorsed golf courses are commonplace. The need to offer "world-class" facilities has pushed the quaint pleasure of desert golf into an anachronistic second place. Originally located some distance from the city, the desert golf club is now surrounded by trucks and earth movers hungrily eyeing up each acre for possible development. The days of Dubai's only eco-friendly golf course (oddly enough it's the lack of any grass that makes it very "green") seem numbered. And it's not only the golf course that is in danger. For in a globalized world of mass communication and travel, the isolated British expat community living far away from home (and the unique customs they create) is also under threat.

One of the more contentious of these quaint traditions from the imperial past was a form of social apartheid, whereby the local people were treated as second-class citizens in their own country. Thesiger described the practice in *Arabian Sands*, while making it clear whose company he preferred:

> *On our way to Dubai we stopped for a night at an oil*
> *camp... bin Kabina and bin Ghabaisha had not been*
> *allowed to share the empty tent which had originally been*
> *allocated to me in the "European lines", and I therefore*
> *spent the night with them in the "native lines".*

Over time, camps such as Thesiger describes put down roots and morphed into residential compounds. One of the most essential elements of this new life was the club, where Indian staff were trained to produce passable fish and chips and mix a decent gin and tonic. Here the long-suffering expat could escape from the local population into an abode of bliss for a few peaceful hours. In less abstemious times, business deals were just as likely to be settled in the club over a few drinks as in the office. But the natives, as is their wont, could be restless. On one compound belonging to the American oil giant Aramco in Saudi Arabia, a riot broke out when the Saudi workers were barred from the cinema used by the expat employees. (Later on the restrictions were reversed, as the Saudi authorities didn't want "locals" mixing with foreigners.)

On the evening I visited the Dubai Country Club, it was clear that the British influence, like its empire before it, had faded considerably. The clientele was 100 percent local, even the snooker table was covered over, in hibernation during the annual heat-induced summer exodus. A group of *shebab* (young Arab men) in white robes played darts, while a few middle-aged men in shorts and polo shirts were sitting at the bar. With Brits in short supply, my companions for the evening became these older gents, a generation now slowly edging their way toward retirement. Sent to the UK in the 1970s for education or training on the first waves of oil money, they returned as engineers or pilots, and occasionally with British wives. As a result of their time abroad, they are often more worldly and speak better English than their children. They are also more comfortable amid the cultural trappings of their former hosts and can speak knowledgeably about Scotland, Wales, or Ireland, distinctions to which younger people in Dubai are often oblivious. Their experiences overseas have even left some of them culturally marooned, caught between their own interpretations of Islam's prohibitions and the more stringent versions currently practiced in much of the Arab world.

Nevertheless, once the conversation turned to politics, any nostalgia these men might have had for their halcyon days in Brighton or Bournemouth quickly faded. The Britain of the twenty-first century was clearly less popular than that of the twentieth. The British Government's readiness to believe that yet *another* war was the perfect solution to the problems afflicting the Middle East was their biggest gripe. As the evening poured on, one of the men beside me reminisced about a driving tour of France he had undertaken from the UK in the 1980s. On the back of his car had been a GB sticker. "Do you know what GB stands for?" he asked, raising his glass in libation. "Go Back British!" His friend piped up with another piece of kindly abuse, "Great Bullshit!"

While theirs was essentially a good-natured ribbing, this wasn't the only anti-British sentiment I encountered during my time exploring Dubai and the rest of the UAE. In a seedy waterfront dive in Ajman, one Emirati became practically apoplectic when talking about the UK and its role in the political affairs of the region. Though the finer points of his argument escaped me, I can still remember the rage in his eyes. It seems that the default setting of "the natives" will always be restlessness. Although if one wants to truly understand where the seeds of such sentiments were sown, the answer lies (as so often) in some little pieces of history it has proven convenient for most people to forget.

🌴

When the first British vessels sailed into the Arabian Gulf in the seventeenth century, they were ships with a one-track mind. Despite the fact that many associate the British Empire's sojourn in Arabia with tales of adventure and heroism – Lawrence of Arabia charging across the desert with his robes and headdress flowing in the wind – there were other, more mercantile, motivations. When the Royal Navy first came calling, it was to secure the lucrative Indo-European trade route that the East India Company used to transfer (some Indians prefer the word "plunder") the natural resources of the subcontinent back to England. Of the two transport options available, a combination of sea and land passing through the Persian Gulf was preferable to a more circuitous sea route around the Cape of Good Hope.

Established by royal charter in 1600, the East India Company was an odd confluence of royal patronage, free enterprise, crony capitalism, and imperial might. The Company enjoyed not only a monopoly on trade in India, but also the right to raise an army and wage war, as the need arose. By the 1700s, the British presence in the subcontinent had become firmly established. The East India Company then morphed into the Government of India; a perfect example of how business and politics are the most conjoined of Siamese twins.

Responsibility for Dubai and the rest of the Gulf fell to this Government of India, the sheikhdoms along the Gulf having closer links with Bombay than Cairo. Thus, representatives were dispatched from India to different ports across the region. The most senior of these was the Political Resident of the Persian Gulf, based in Busheir on the Persian side of the Gulf. The Political Resident was backed up by a number of lower-ranking political agents in smaller ports such as Dubai and Sharjah. These imperial representatives spent a lot of time coming to an understanding of the local people and culture, even if they sought this knowledge primarily to pursue the interests of the Crown more effectively. By studying the intricate tribal allegiances at work within the ruling families, they often played opposing factions off against one another.

In time, by cajoling and prodding the local sheikhs to pursue policies that favored the British, these political agents became the most influential figures in the region. The level of control the British Empire exerted over the local rulers was astounding. The political agent dictated who the local rulers could talk to, what countries they could visit, even what kind of goods could be imported into each princely domain. Opposition was infrequent and gentle reminders were generally sufficient to keep this important avenue of trade ticking along nicely. Occasionally, a sheikh might pursue policies that a political agent thought unproductive, and a warship might be dispatched to the home port of the sheikh in question. If his truculence continued, a few broadsides of gunboat diplomacy usually changed his mind. Normally the Arab sheikhs deferred to the superior firepower of the British, though there were some who occasionally cried *non serviam!*

In the eighteenth century, Dubai was an insignificant little town of less than 1,000 people. Long before the Maktoums had established their dynasty in Dubai, it was the Al Qasimi tribe who ruled the roost along these shores. From their base in Ras Al Khaimah, their control extended across all the northern emirates of the present-day UAE (Fujairah, Ajman, Um Al Quwain, and Sharjah) and even across the pond to some ports in today's Iran. At this point in history, the Al Qasimi clan was undoubtedly top dog (to use a culturally insensitive turn of phrase) in these parts.

However, the Gulf wasn't broad enough for two Big Kahunas. By the beginning of the nineteenth century the Royal Navy had made the British Empire the world's undisputed superpower. Historians have described the Gulf at the time as a "British lake" where Her Majesty's wishes reigned supreme. And once the Al Qasimi clan and the East India Company came into competition over the shipping of goods from India through the Gulf, things were never going to end prettily. The East India Company cried foul and began to blame the Al Qasimis for every act of seaborne buccaneering in the lower Gulf. The deteriorating relationship between the British and Ras Al Khaimah was exacerbated by the staunchly anti-imperialist stance of the Al Qasimis. This was inspired in part by their Wahhabist reading of Islam, which was popular in some parts of the Arabian Peninsula at this time and is still the official state doctrine of Saudi Arabia. Founded by the Saudi religious cleric Muhammad Ibn Abd al-Wahhab in the eighteenth century, Wahhabism was an ultra-conservative religious-political movement based on a literal reading of the Koran. This interpretation of Islamic doctrine depicted nonbelievers such as the British as a corrupting presence that Arabia would be better off without.

Things came to a head when some British ships were attacked, men and women kidnapped, and some unfortunates forced to convert to Islam under extreme duress. After an initial British raid in 1809 failed to quell the piracy, the Government of India decided to act more decisively in 1819. A British Navy fleet was dispatched and destroyed the Al Qasimi fleet of 300 ships and much of the town with a bombardment that lasted three days. The good relations that Abu Dhabi (and its then dependency of Dubai) maintained with the British meant that it remained untouched.

Wiping out their fleet destroyed the Al Qasimis' wealth and power in one swoop, a blow from which Ras Al Khaimah and its ruling family have never fully recovered. This attack by the Royal Navy set in motion the gradual decline of a once mighty clan. In the aftermath of this destruction, the British signed agreements with Sharjah, Um Al Quwain, Ajman, and Fujairah, allowing them to become independent sheikhdoms in their own right. The subsequent succession of treaties and truces also led to a change in the regional nomenclature. The Pirate Coast became known as the Trucial Coast. In such situations you see exactly how fluid history can be, how all of our tomorrows are eternally being reinvented by decisions and actions taken today. Without the interference of the British, what might have happened? Rather than being broken up into impotent little emirates, there could have been an expansive, tumid Ras Al Khaimah state (along the lines of Saudi Arabia) instead of the UAE. Centuries later, it is Dubai that has grabbed the limelight and has its name heralded across the globe.

Given this military clout, there is no doubt that all the sheikhs along the Gulf coast would have feared incurring Her Majesty's displeasure. Yet this was a reciprocal relationship, and as long as the rulers bowed to the will of London on external affairs, they could count on the support of the Royal Navy when internal difficulties arose. In 1934, when a breakaway clan of the ruling family threatened the rule of the Maktoum dynasty, the Royal Navy dispatched a gunboat to sit off the coast. Sheikh Said was invited on board and a shipment of weapons was brought ashore in daylight to let the local population know that *al Hakam* had the backing of the Crown.

But by the 1960s, the special relationships that existed between the UK and its protectorates along the Gulf had run their course. Even in the late 1940s, Thesiger's writings contain hints about the eventual unwinding of the special position the British had once occupied across the region, such as the growing closeness between Saudi Arabia and American oil companies. One of Britain's last colonial acts along the Trucial Coast was to assist Sheikh Zayed of Abu Dhabi in overthrowing his brother in a bloodless coup in 1966.

In 1968, the British Government definitively announced its intention to withdraw from its territories east of Suez. Proud Arab nationalists insist that the Gulf sheikhs were only too keen to see the back of the British and cast aside their colonial yokes, though the reality was very different. Sheikh Zayed of Abu Dhabi even offered US$4.25 million to pay for the continued presence of British soldiers. Fear was his main motivation in asking the British to stay. Abu Dhabi was sitting on top of a bucketful of oil and, despite the protestations of Arab unity popular at the time, Sheikh Zayed obviously didn't trust his neighbors. His request would prove to be prescient a couple of decades later when Iraqi tanks rolled into Kuwait. Of course, Saddam Hussein's attempt to redraw the borders of the region and give Iraq a 19th province was done in the spirit of "brotherly" Arab relations.

When Her Majesty's Government finally withdrew from the Gulf, facilitating the establishment of the United Arab Emirates in 1971, the special relationship that existed prior to its departure didn't simply disappear. Even after nationhood was achieved, a number of British expatriates continued to play an important role in the affairs of the UAE. Many simply swapped their military or diplomatic roles for senior positions in the private sector. Such

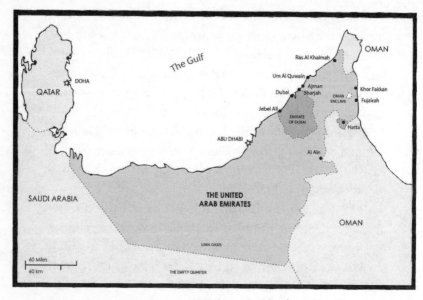

arrangements were common across Arabia. In Oman, a group of former British military men exercised not inconsiderable influence over the Sultan in the 1970s and 1980s. One former British officer even earned the tag the "White Sultan" because of his closeness to the Omani ruler. This was allegedly attained due to his involvement in a coup that saw Sultan Qaboos oust his own father. Blood may be thicker than water, but it's not as viscous as oil.

Today, this postcolonial narrative has been laid to rest in Dubai. To a large extent, the emirate has cast off the imperial chip that sits uncomfortably on the shoulder of so many of its neighbors. Anyway, times change and British gunboats no longer rule the waves. As the balance of power in the Gulf has ebbed and flowed, so have the allegiances of these former British protectorates. Jebel Ali port is now a home from home for the aircraft carriers, frigates, and cruisers of the US Navy as Dubai has cuddled up to the latest stick-wielding superpower to come sailing up the Gulf.

5
The Best City in India

IT'S A FRIDAY MORNING and I'm standing at the Sabkha *abra* station along the Creek, a raucous gathering of human traffic. A waterborne version of the London Underground, the *abra* is the traditional way to make one's way back and forth across the Creek, though engines coughing out pungent black fumes have long since replaced oars and sweat as the means of propulsion. Incoming and outgoing boats bounce off each other like bumper cars as they dock, while ships' captains harangue and corral passengers down the gangplanks toward their empty boats. Regular commuters from across the Asian subcontinent step deftly on and off each boat, while tourists teeter uncertainly as each *abra* bobs back and forth in the water. On a busy morning, driving from one side of the city to the other could take an hour, but by water the passage is complete in minutes. And despite the commotion when coming aboard, crossing the Creek with twenty other passengers bathed in the morning sun is never anything but a pleasure.

Although the journey is brief, it feels as if you have traveled considerably further when you disembark on the other side. Walking under a long covered street past shops such as Jaipur Trading, you are teleported far across the Arabian Sea. This is the Old Souk, which for some time has been a focus for the city's most populous expatriate community, the Non-Resident Indians (NRI). While the Maktoums and other local families are keen to accentuate the city's Arabian heritage and British expatriates still exercise considerable influence, Indian citizens and their culture are by far the most pervasive. As such, Dubai moves not to the lilting refrain of an Arabic *oud* (lute) but to a *tabla* beat, a Hindustani rhythm you can feel pulsating throughout the city.

Dubai is the prime conduit through which Indian expatriates interface with the region, exchanging both knowledge and sweat for hard currency. But all the countries along the Arabian Gulf share a long history with India. While the spice trade brought Arabs to India, pearls brought Indians to the Gulf. Pearls harvested from these shallow waters were sold to India and in return came many of the essentials of everyday life. There were spices for cooking, wood for shipbuilding, silks and cottons for *kanduras* and *abayas*, even gold to stockpile one's fortune. Until the era of oil, the balance of power in this relationship was very much in favor of India, a country teeming with raw materials, financial clout, and ancient learning; and until the introduction of the UAE dirham after independence, the Indian rupee was a common unit of currency. India was so important to the merchants in the Gulf that a family member often lived permanently along the western coast of India to facilitate this trade. Such was the depth of the relationship that over time Arabs even acquired the family name Al-Hindi; in the Old Souk, one establishment still bears that name.

Despite the depth of this relationship, by the beginning of the twentieth century there were only about 50 Indian families residing in what was still a minor port town. And in the days before Indian independence and partition, the word "Indian" had a far broader meaning, as Pakistan had not yet come into existence. In colonial times, these Indians would have enjoyed high status. Not only were they entitled to protection as British subjects and representatives of British business interests, many were also successful merchants in their own right. When India gained independence from Britain in 1947, Dubai became even more attractive for Indian businessmen. As the new Indian Government adopted protectionist economic policies, opportunities arose to exploit price differentials in gold and textiles between Dubai and India.

It was only in the 1960s and 1970s that Indians began to arrive by the *lakh*. Thousands upon thousands of barbers, shopkeepers, manual laborers, clerks, bookkeepers, and cooks, along with a considerable number of doctors, accountants, and engineers, began to swell the ranks of Dubai's labor force, which in turn gave much of the city a distinctly Indian feel. This pattern has continued to the present day. The figures speak for themselves: out of a population of around two million, the last available statistics had Indians accounting for an estimated 43 percent of the total, or 51 percent of all expatriates. If this were in the days of the Raj (when India stretched from Karachi in Pakistan to Dhaka in Bangladesh), "Indians" would make up a staggering 68 percent of Dubai's population. Throw in illegal immigrants or undocumented workers and it could break the 70 percent mark.

Yet numbers alone cannot convey the extent to which all things Indian have seeped into the pores of the city. For India is an envelopment of the senses (the more fragile may say an assault) and in the streets around the Old Souk, all five are caressed with something approaching the vigor one might expect in *Bharat* herself. Women resplendent in brightly hued saris test the quality of silk, discussing prices in Malayalam and Gujarati, while nearby cafés offer impeccable *masala chai* and fill the air with the aroma of *pakoras* and other savory treats for any NRI in need of refreshment and a taste of home.

There is also spiritual sustenance on offer. At one end of the Old Souk, behind the textile shops and beside the water, a serpentine queue of Indians, young and old, winds around some of the older buildings. I stand and watch for a while. Shoes are removed as people join the ever-expanding line, standing patiently in the morning sun. I ask one of those waiting what's going on. "*Puja*," he replies. The need for further explanation disappears once I catch sight of a man emerging from an alley with a dash of red *kum kum* powder on his forehead, marking the spot where Dubai diverges from many of its neighbors.

This little warren of alleyways is home to a Hindu temple honoring Shiva, the destroyer of evil, its rough, stooped walls reassuringly ignoring the right angles that dominate so much of the city's architecture. As it is Friday morning, these narrow streets are crowded with devotees and security guards are deployed to keep the tight pack moving in an orderly flow. In Dubai the weekend runs from Friday to Saturday, the former being the Islamic Sabbath. Thus by default, Friday is the main day for communal prayer for Hindus and Christians as well.

On one narrow street, a line of colorful little shops sell a pantheon of Hindu paraphernalia. There are statues of the elephant-headed Ganesh (the remover of obstacles), CDs carrying an assortment of *bhagans* (devotional Indian music), and individual *puja* kits, flowers, milk, and a coconut delicately arranged in a basket, the traditional offerings made during prayer. Though the red sands of Arabia are nearby, this is a scene that wouldn't look out of place in Varanasi, one of India's holiest cities on the banks of the river Ganges; all that is missing is a cow or two gently ambling by. Above all, the smells and colors add to the sense of dislocation – lavender mixed with incense, fresh water still clutching to the flowers misting up the air as marigold orange and cool blue lotus collide in a fusion of hues. The walls are bedecked with posters advertising a host of ancillary services for the practicing Hindu: astrologers, matchmakers, and *vastu shastra* experts (an Indian *feng shui*) who offer guidance in the pursuit of "peace, prosperity and happiness."

As the crowds continue to pass through, my attention is caught by two men descending a flight of stairs from the temple above. One is wearing a vivid orange turban and carrying a bright pink cushion on his head, on which lies a magnificent pearl necklace. The other is similarly turbaned, but gently wafting a large white feather over the delicately arranged pearls. Forming a two-man religious procession, they pass in front of me and then head out of the alley into the adjoining streets. I follow. After a short distance, the pilgrims' progress ends in a nearby street beyond the temple complex, where a Mercedes four-wheel drive is waiting to receive the mendicants. The pillow and the necklace are religiously placed on someone's lap before the vehicle whisks them away.

I didn't understand exactly what I'd seen, but I was intrigued nonetheless. Inquisitiveness propelled me back into the alley and up the stairs to the temple overhead. In contrast to the relative austerity of Sunni mosques, this was a technicolor spirituality. The Hindu faithful moved in a continual procession past brightly painted statues, offerings gifts of milk, while others knelt and prostrated themselves on the ground in supplication. Another flight of stairs led upward to a *gurmandir*, a prayer room whose walls were lined with paintings of gray-bearded gurus. At one end of the room a large, ornately inscribed book (presumably the Vedas, the sacred Sanskrit scriptures of Hinduism) was positioned on a raised platform-cum-altar. A steady line of devotees approached to take a blessing, by either touching the portraits of the gurus or wafting their hands over the small brass lamps burning coconut oil. Of all these, one remained in my mind for a long time after: a young mother with a newborn clutched close to her chest, walking in slow, deliberate circles around this gathering of holy books, seeking a blessing and good fortune for this latest addition to the community that most defines Dubai.

By the time I descended the stairs to the streets below, I felt a greater understanding of why Dubai holds such a strong appeal for Indian émigrés. Despite the fact that millions of Indians live and work across the Gulf region, the freedom to perform their daily devotions openly is often denied to Hindus. And the fact that all these expressions of faith occurred literally in the shadow of the Grand Mosque is testament to one of Dubai's most appealing characteristics: its openness, especially as less tolerant interpretations of Islam are currently in vogue.

Saudi Arabia is loath to let any religion other than Islam bare its face in public, forcing people to use secret temples instead. An Indian friend once described how Hindus are forced to worship in an "underground" temple in Kuwait, as they fear incurring the displeasure of the country's religious fundamentalists. He said: "I didn't particularly enjoy the feeling of being in the 'temple' in Kuwait. It was quite furtive and guerrilla-like. I prefer my spirituality to be less constrained. I definitely resented being in a country where my religion and way of life are illegal. That is definitely suffocating. A large part of the Indian population likes to visit temples and will definitely feel constrained if they can't do so freely."

Another Hindu businessman living in Dubai recounted how he disliked traveling to Saudi Arabia on business, as customs officials in the kingdom are notoriously fussy about the importation of any religious items pertaining to any faith other than Islam. The intolerance preached by some Islamic scholars toward Hinduism (and even toward fellow Muslims of other denominations) is an oppressive burden under which to live.

But Dubai has little time for such narrow-mindedness and the adage "be happy in your work" has certainly been embraced by the powers that be. Anyway, no amount of theological squabbling can detract from the sheer size of the Indian community. Given that the crowds who assemble for prayers every Friday at both the temple and the nearby mosque are predominantly Indian, these are people who would have grown up in an atmosphere of religious diversity, if not always tolerance. As another Indian expat quipped: "Where are the Emiratis who might object to all this?" He had a point. Looking around the streets that morning there wasn't a *kandura* in sight.

By now the crowd had begun to disperse and I followed the departing devotees to the Creek and boarded an *abra* back to Deira. The Indian man sitting beside me still had the distinctive red *kum kum* mark on his forehead. After a few opening pleasantries, I asked him if Hindus face any problems conducting their religious ceremonies so publicly. Were there any objections? In response, he intertwined his fingers and said that Muslims, Christians, and Hindus all got along well together, while giving Dubai, as a whole, the thumbs up. As if to support his point, he pointed to the only Arab on board, sitting on my right. This older man stood out from the rest of the passengers. Short in stature, he had the wiry build often associated with people whose ancestors were the original inhabitants of the Arabian Peninsula. His white hair was the same colour as his simple robe and headdress. The fabric was not the fine material you would associate with a chic Dubai local, so I assumed he was an Omani or an out-of-towner from the outlying Emirates. He looked uncomfortable, and his eyes moved somewhat nervously from side to side as we motored back through the water. Amid the young Indian men joking and laughing in the morning sun, *he* was the one who looked out of place.

It is not merely opportunities to enrich one's soul that make this town such a go-to destination for would-be Indian expats with expansive dreams. There are substantial material benefits to leaving one's homeland and relocating to the other side of the Arabian Sea. First of all, the purchasing power of a Dubai salary when remitted to India is staggering. In a single bound, a young Indian software engineer who lands a position at a multinational company can leapfrog years, if not generations, of economic advancement. Despite the achievements India has aggregated since independence, hundreds of millions still live in conditions of extreme poverty. Along the roadsides of India you can find families living under black tarpaulins, working on government road projects. These schemes employ men and women to spend their days using large stones to break smaller ones into pebbles. For such people, escape is often no more than a dream. But if they do manage to emigrate, there is a chance for some of India's poor to transcend their *karma* in Dubai.

Of all the Indian communities in the city, Malayalis (people who hail from the southern state of Kerala) are the most numerous. Despite its relatively small size and population (only 30 million), Kerala has one of the best education systems in India, and its high school and college graduates are in great demand across the Gulf. Its high literacy rates are generally attributed to the fact that Kerala has one of world's few democratically elected Communist governments. While the Communist Party of India's many years in power have produced a revolution in education, this is still not enough to keep everyone at home. Thus Keralites from all walks of life are cornerstones of Dubai's economy. And the dirhams these émigrés remit to their home state each month are a vital part of Kerala's economy as well.

In ten years, a taxi driver or barber should be able to save up enough money to build a house back home in Thiruvananthapuram. On his return, an industrious driver can then enjoy a standard of living that only a professional, businessman, or crook could afford. Notwithstanding the material benefits, this is a lonely life, however. One Keralan taxi driver told me how he had sacrificed his life on the altar of the dirham for fifteen years by living alone as a bachelor while his family remained in India. For him, the deprivation was worth it. His children received an education that would have been impossible had he remained at home. His daughter qualified as a nurse and now she also had the option to emigrate. But her education (funded from Dubai) had expanded her horizons even further than her father's to include Australia or Canada.

The importance of the relationship between Dubai and Kerala can only be truly grasped by visiting a Keralan city such as Cochin. At a Western Union office in the bustling Ernakulam district, you can see an advertisement featuring a picture of the Burj Al Arab, with an Indian man looking wistfully into the distance. The image below shows a much younger-looking woman with a child, beaming broadly to the camera as they open a Western Union envelope with their latest remittance from the Gulf. The deeper message is simple to grasp: a move to Dubai equals money, a beautiful wife, and healthy kids – all which of equals success.

Yet this is still not enough. For many Indians, Dubai is only the first port of call on a well-worn path of global migration. This is a road that leads Indian émigrés first to the Gulf and then in time to Canada, the USA, the UK, or Australia. You see the same ads for immigration lawyers printed all across the Gulf, promising a better life in the West. Even if an Indian lives in Dubai for fifty years, neither he nor his children qualify for UAE citizenship and the privilege that comes with it. This is especially true for the middle classes who do not own their own businesses and are dependent on the goodwill of others to make a living. The vast discrepancies in wealth one sees in India are replicated within the community's expat population. If you exist on the lower rungs of the social ladder in India, there's a good chance you'll end up in the same place in Dubai, even if you are better off financially. Also, many Indians covet western passports so that they can leave and immediately return earning two or three times their salary for doing the exact same job; a western passport opens a lot of closed doors.

Nevertheless, unlike back home in India, there are few power cuts in Dubai. Though the air is dusty at times, it is free from that noxious black smoke that can rip through your child's lungs. The water that comes through the pipes is safe to drink, while TB, malaria, and a host of other nasty diseases are not endemic. While stopped at a traffic light, a leper will not tap a stump against the window of your car looking for spare change. The authorities do not have "encounters" with criminals; police death squads in India routinely save the nation the bother of a trial by dispatching criminals to the great hereafter with a bullet in the head.

And across the city each weekend, the Indian community gets to live out its bespoke edition of the Dubai dream. Mothers stroll through the gold shops in the Mina Bazaar selecting wedding ensembles for their daughters.

Vegetarians dine on South Indian *thali*, while all-rounders can consume Moghul meat curries or mulligatawny soup. There are even eateries offering special preparations for those who adhere to the Jain religion, an offshoot of Hinduism whose adherents eschew onions, garlic, and potatoes. (The prohibition on the humble spud may explain why Jains are rather thin on the ground in Ireland.) On India's national day, the shops are festooned with the horizontal green, white, and orange bars of the national flag.

With the working week done, Dubai has a chance to gleam, a jewel of Asia shining like a beacon to hundreds of millions of impoverished Indians across the Arabian Sea. Families gather alongside the Creek to picnic and play cricket; a full selection of Bollywood films play in the cinemas; and *desi* promotions at the city's nightclubs allow bright young Indian things to dance the night away to *bhangra* (traditional Indian music hooked up to an electronic beat), living it up in what has become, for some, the best city in India.

6

Bringing the Mountain

BOTH ASHRAF AND HIS MOUSTACHE were getting very animated as he leaned forward from the back seat and summed up his argument. For the last ten minutes, this well-spoken Pakistani businessman had been loudly castigating the American government for not appreciating the losses his countrymen were enduring as they took the fight to the Taliban in the border regions of his homeland near Afghanistan. I was in the front passenger seat, watching the driver (decked out in an Emirati *kandura*) from the tour company raise his eyes to heaven in time with the crescendos of Ashraf's stinging criticisms. Despite the variety of political opinions that no doubt existed within the vehicle, for the time being we were all fellow travelers, journeying out of the city to engage in that quintessential Dubai tourist experience, the desert safari.

When oil reserves began drying up in the 1990s, it was to the renewable resource of tourism that the Maktoums looked in order to bankroll the dream. Yet there is a certain incongruity in this ambition to be a global tourist destination. Dubai is certainly not a place of great natural beauty. Much of the emirate is rather modest, low-lying desert, with some taller dunes outside the city. Nor does it possess an ancient culture: when the Maktoum family established the ruling line in the 1830s (after a subtribe of the Bani Yas broke away from neighboring Abu Dhabi), Dubai was little more than an impoverished fishing village. My experiences so far, which had been primarily restricted to foreigners, seemed to confirm one often-repeated criticism thrown at the city by its detractors. Culture vultures are quick to dis-

miss Dubai as a plastic Arabia that has lost its identity, overwhelmed by foreign influences and immigration. For anyone with a fetish for the Arabia of the past, for Ali Baba and
A *Thousand and One Nights*, Dubai thus throws up numerous obstacles. The desert safari promised a real Arabian
Night and I wanted to experience it at first hand.

Practically every hotel has a desk flogging the "ultimate" Dubai experience to all comers. Although the dip-
tych of desert and safari may not seem like the most
natural of bedfellows, necessity has forced the city to be
creative when it comes to entertaining its guests. A
brochure at my hotel listed some of the cultural highlights
that lay before us:

Picture with Falcon
Enchanting Belly Dancing Show
Barbecue Veg/Non Veg
Arabic Tea/Coffee
Dune Bashing
Camel Riding
Photograph in Local Dresses
Henna Painting (for ladies only)

A cultural kaleidoscope of *Arabia Felix* was promised,
though vegetarianism is not the first thing that springs to
mind when I play association games with the word
Arabian; my mind is more likely to conjure up mountains
of skewered meat. Yet the unfettered predaciousness common in the Gulf has been tempered somewhat by Dubai's
large Hindu population. It is not uncommon to see restaurants with signs unashamedly announcing to the world
that they are Pure Veg.

Beside Ashraf was another Pakistani man; the two of
them were partners in a construction business and were in

town for the week mixing business with pleasure. In their sixties, they both spoke in the crisp, measured tones reminiscent of BBC broadcasters from the 1950s; their sentences were liberally peppered with words like "fellow" and "chap." Creased trousers and pressed shirts were their uniform of choice. Sartorial balance was only restored after we stopped at a youth hostel in the Al Qusais area to squeeze the last two guests (a Moroccan woman and a young Englishman) into the back seats. From there, we proceeded to a rendezvous point outside the city, where a number of tour operators had congregated, before caravanning en masse to the desert.

Careering around the desert in a four-wheel drive was a favored pastime of the western oil men, nurses, and teachers who came to the Gulf in the 1970s and 1980s (there was precious little else to do), but in Dubai dune bashing has been transposed into a must-do cultural experience. If the terrain includes mountain valleys and dried-out river beds, the term *wadi* bashing is used. Never afraid to move with the times, dune boarding has also been incorporated as an optional extra and it is also very much a Dubai activity. This involves strapping a snowboard to your feet (thankfully after being driven to the top of a sand dune) and then careering back down again, as fast as the sand can carry you. My first experience of the sport involved a few seconds of graceful flight, before I ended up face first in a pile of hot sand.

I didn't get long to wallow in my thoughts of authenticity and simulation, as Ashraf was still firing on all cylinders behind me. His latest assertion was that America had tossed money and guns into the cooking pot of Afghan politics in the 1980s, but then left the whole thing to burn on the stove during the 1990s – a culinary *faux pas* with grievous geopolitical ramifications. The longer he talked, the louder his condemnations of the US became, and before long he began sticking the boot into perfidious Albion as well. Ashraf insisted that neither the Americans nor anybody else would ever get a definitive result fighting the tribes on either side of the Afghan–Pakistan border. "The Pathans are natural warriors. They have a rifle in their hand from birth!" was his preferred cliché to describe his fellow countrymen, while citing previous failings by the British and the Russians to suppress armed opposition to their presence. Despite the vehemence in his voice, Ashraf struck me as a realist rather than a sophist. For the duration of his speech, the two newcomers had remained very silent in the back. I presumed that an impromptu lecture on international relations and insurgency suppression hadn't been mentioned in their brochure.

By now the city had slipped away and the desert stepped forward to envelop us. The empty expanses looked uninviting and the sand-filled sky had taken on the hue of dirty dishwater. Whoever came up with the idea of turning Dubai into a global tourism center must have been an optimist. When we stopped for a few moments to stretch our legs, the driver encouraged us all to get out and take some snapshots against the obligatory backdrop of desert sunset. As the twilight drew in, I spotted Ashraf and his friend posing for photographs and offered to take one of them together. As they stood side by side, the pair looked rather rigid. So in a serious voice I called out, "Say God Bless America!" For a moment there was no reaction, but just as the shutter closed they both burst into laughter, capturing them for posterity in the midst of the biggest belly laugh I'd seen in some time.

The stop seemed to have had a calming effect on Ashraf. Once we were moving again, the conversation gradually turned from politics to tourism, but he still couldn't get off the subject of his homeland. "Have you ever been to Pakistan? It is one of the most beautiful countries in the world. Every year there is a polo match at 12,000 feet in the mountains between Gilgit and Chitral in Shandur. Can you imagine it?" he said.

Though Ashraf was a captivating speaker, I was experiencing a modicum of frustration. I had wanted the safari to be an Arabian experience, a contrast to the city itself, where the influence of the Indian subcontinent can at times suffocate the local Arab culture, but the dearth of Arabs was making this objective a tad difficult. Even the driver wearing the *kandura* was fake. He was in fact an Iranian and only wore the robe when driving tourists around. Presumably it added an air of legitimacy to the proceedings. Despite my reservations, I decided to give in and embrace the reality around me, regardless of any demographic discrepancies.

Ashraf became even more rapturous as he described the beauty of the mountainous north of his homeland. He painted a picture of snow-topped peaks and crystal-blue lakes, an earthly paradise if ever there was one. All this was a world away from the overcast dustbowl outside. Given the cards Dubai has been dealt, I couldn't help but be impressed by the spin doctors behind the emirate's reinvention as a tourist destination. Dubai had focused on the other things that twenty-first-century tourists crave: safety, shopping, and ease of access. Emirates Airlines had made the city reachable from six continents and tourist visas are available on arrival. It would take a lot more than good marketing to sell Taliban tourism to the world.

When the driver slammed his foot on the accelerator and charged up a tall red sand dune, throwing us all back into

our seats, we knew that the "bashing" had begun. After gun-
ning up and down the first few dunes, the Moroccan woman
declared she felt nauseous and asked to sit in the front. We
stopped, got out, and I climbed in the back beside the young
Englishman. Following fifteen minutes of being rattled
around like maracas, we arrived at the top of a dune over-
looking a camp, the venue for the evening's entertainment.
As the convoy of twenty or so vehicles disgorged its passengers, I saw just how wide Dubai's tourist net is thrown. A host
of Chinese, Indians, Arabs, Europeans, Africans, and
Americans spewed forth into the warm night. There was
even a Saudi man (in a white robe and red-checked headdress) accompanied by his wife, her face and figure concealed
behind a black *niqab* and *abaya* respectively. I wondered what
part of the desert safari they had come to see.

The first activity was having your picture taken on top
of a camel. If you chose to mount the beast, the camel was
walked ten yards in one direction, before the handler
turned around and walked back – an Arabian version of a
Blackpool pony ride. While this entertained the kids (and
quite a few adults), the young Englishman, who went by
the name of Haines, wasn't impressed. "Tourist trap," was
all he said, shaking his head. Such stage-managed events
weren't part of the authentic travel experience he had
planned. "Usually I avoid things like this," he added,
somewhat apologetically. From the crest of the dune we
proceeded downward to the camp. Haines had only
recently graduated from university and had a good job
lined up for the autumn. In the meantime, he was flying
to Australia to see some friends. For this young man, the
right-of-passage gap year had been condensed into a gap
month. He was visiting Australia and New Zealand with
stopovers in Dubai and Bangkok – enough traveling to last
some people a lifetime.

Inside the camp Arabic coffee and dates were on offer, but these were bypassed by the tourists; most contented themselves with the free Pepsi until the barbecue was ready. Once we were fed, I sipped on some coffee and tried to ignore the thumping rap music the sound system was pumping out. Relief only arrived when the familiar strings of an Arabic love song floated over the camp. This was the signal that the main event was at hand. Everyone sat around a raised square platform as a pale, raven-haired woman readied herself at the side. It was time for the belly dancing to begin.

Ever since Salome convinced King Herod to lop off the head of John the Baptist, women cavorting to rhythmic beats have generated a significant amount of discussion in this part of the world. Recalling that dancing in public is *haram* (forbidden) in Saudi Arabia, I finally understood the attraction for the Saudi couple. Even in the spiritual home of the belly dance, the hip-shaking women of Egypt have undergone censure in both the distant and recent past. At one time, belly dancers were even barred from exposing their bellies. This prohibition led to the use of a sheer piece of material to cover, yet not conceal, the offending anatomical feature. Nowadays, 90 percent of such dancers in Dubai are from the former Soviet Union. A similar "Red Dawn" in Cairo became such a contentious issue that the government imposed a ban on foreign dancers in 2005.

As the dancer took center stage, she moved her hips in time to the tick-tock of the music, a Middle Eastern metronome that had the audience truly engaged for the first time that evening. Certainly there was something hypnotic about her movements and I felt some sympathy for poor old Gustave Flaubert. He has taken a beating in some intellectual circles over the years, after falling for an

Egyptian belly dancer named Kuchuk Hanem during his travels in the Middle East. Nevertheless, unlike the belly dancing one might see in Cairo, Dubai has taken a more *Hi-Di-Hi* approach to this favored form of entertainment. Five minutes into her act, the dancer dragged six men (Haines and I included) to the center of the stage. For good measure, she lifted up our t-shirts and tied them above our waists, all the time encouraging us to mimic her movements. Despite the dancer's best encouragement, my own hips refused to move in time with the music and reverted to the atavistic state of discombobulation etched deep in the DNA of most Irishmen.

It was while standing there that I felt an epiphany descend from on high. My search for authenticity (here at least) was as misguided and foolish as I no doubt looked at that particular moment. Belly dancing is in fact an import to Dubai, with no place in the traditional Bedouin culture, as indicative of Arabia as flamenco dancing is of England. That said, there was no point taking such setbacks too seriously – even Haines was enjoying himself now. I also began to understand some of the reasons behind Dubai's success in selling itself to the world. It gives its visitors *A Thousand and One Nights* in one easy package. The dancing gives you a little flavor of Morocco, Turkey, and Egypt while the grilled kebabs and hummus let you taste the cuisine of Israel, Palestine, Lebanon, and Syria. And it all takes place against the backdrop of the Arabian Desert and the famed hospitality of the Gulf. Authenticity be damned!

Five minutes later it was the women's turn to join in the humiliation, though they proved to have a greater anatomical aptitude for the dancing than the men. When the last of the amateurs had been paraded, the professional took over and gave a virtuoso performance. Half an hour later, the safari was finished and it was time to go.

As we drove back to the city, I tried to put the evening and my time in Dubai so far into some kind of perspective. The myriad of nationalities you can meet on any given day in Dubai is disorienting and generates peculiar sensations. For some reason, a scene from the science fiction film *Event Horizon* summarizes my understanding best. An engineer has to explain to the bemused crew of a spaceship exactly how he overcame the niggling difficulty of designing a vessel that could travel faster than the speed of light. To do so, he holds up a centerfold from a twenty-third-century girlie magazine and explains that conventionally, the shortest distance between two points is a straight line. However, for his QED moment, he simply folds the two ends together while declaring: "The shortest distance between two points is zero!" When it comes to the art of travel, Dubai manages to perform a similar sleight of hand. In this instance it had indeed folded space, literally bringing the mountain to us. In Dubai, a busy tourist or businessman can stop over for a day or two and get a nonthreatening introduction to Arabia.

Despite the convenience, there is something disconcerting about such an experience. I wondered what someone like Dervla Murphy – a prodigious Irish traveler and writer who peddled her bike full tilt from Dublin to Delhi in the 1960s – might make of such a twenty-first-century approach to travel. I also felt that Dubai's scattergun inclusiveness was out of control and in danger of overloading my palate. There were still so many things I didn't know about Dubai, yet I had learned about the workings of a Hindu temple and the spare parts business in West Africa. I knew where to get some of the best lamb this side of Kabul (the Afghan Kebab House in Naif) or vegetarian food that wouldn't offend a Jain, yet where were the restaurants serving Gulf specialties such as *matchboose*, *harees*, or *ouzi*? By bringing together so many snippets of disparate cultures, I feared that Dubai was offering a weak and insipid brew to the thirsty traveler, full of the ephemeral fizz of a Pepsi but with none of the bitter, lasting sensations of real Arabic coffee. And amid all this concrete, aluminum, and glass, I sometimes felt completely lost; often Dubai doesn't even feel like the Middle East. You search in vain for something to remind you of the desolate Martian moonscapes of Oman or the all-enveloping, seeping history of Damascus.

There is something akin to a magician's trick about Dubai. You know it's not real, but it grabs your attention nonetheless. I was still wondering where the reality was.

7
From a Doodle to a Theme Park

WHAT WOULD LEONARDO DA VINCI MAKE OF THIS? Hanging on the wall in front of me was a large reproduction of the *Mona Lisa*, though the Florentine's famous smile was concealed behind a gold *burqa*, the falcon-inspired face mask that is traditionally worn by older women in the UAE and Oman. (The Emirati *burqa* should not be confused with the over-the-head, body-covering tarpaulin preferred by Taliban fashionistas in Afghanistan.) But this amendment to Da Vinci's original was not the work of a censorious artist affronted by the sight of a lady's face; this was satire, Dubai style.

The location was Dubai Media City (DMC). I had come to meet an Emirati man called Mohammed, the creator of a hit animated television show called *Freej*. The offices of his production company were stylishly outfitted, befitting a fledgling, ambitious media concern. After my frustrations on the desert excursion, I felt the need for some real Arabia, no matter how modern.

Mohammed was dressed in a *kandura* and a baseball cap, a perfect fusion of East and West. Like many young people of his generation, he had been sent abroad to study in order to acquire some useful skill to bring back for the greater development of his homeland. But Dubai got a little more than it bargained for. "I went to the US to study architecture but I hated it!" he said. "Back then, if you went to study in the States, people thought you were crazy if you didn't study something important, like engineering or medicine." However, a chance encounter in the Art Department one day set him on a different path. "I saw this 'Introduction to Animation' class and straightway changed my major to Art. A few weeks later, for an assignment, our lecturer told us we had to draw a superhero based on somebody or something we knew. I was stuck. All I had in my notebook were some doodles of old Emirati women wearing the *burqa*. But then I thought, 'Why can't a grandmother be a superhero?'"

Mohammed explained the source of his inspiration. In the past, Dubai had relied heavily on the pearl industry as a source of income. This was grueling seasonal work, as the *ghous* (diving season) unfortunately corresponded with the hottest months of the year. Each summer, the men would sail off down the Gulf to the pearling banks, where they dived without oxygen and gathered the pearl oysters by hand. The life these pearl divers led is still documented in sea shanties and maritime museums, but there is little information about what life was like for the women left behind to take care of the house and children.

Yet that is not surprising. In the large volume of writing that exists on the people and culture of Arabia, women are often reduced to shadowy figures, slipping in and out of the narratives woven by those who traveled through the region. And as most of the literature on Arabia has been written by men, one can read lengthy volumes and yet learn precious little about the fairer half of the population, even today. The inherent limitations to which all foreigners must succumb when writing about a different culture are magnified for men in the Gulf, as traditionally half of the population are largely out of bounds. It is often foreign women who marry into Arab families who have the fullest understanding of what really goes on behind closed doors. Their impressions tend to be less rose-tinted as well.

Freej, in its own way, goes some way toward filling out the other side of the ledger, which has been conspicuously empty over the years. The show, in its own words, is simply about "four old biddies sitting around talking about nothing." Though devised and scripted by a man, the story is told from the perspective of local people who would have experienced this often hidden part of their culture at first hand, while sitting on their granny's knee. One of the things I liked about *Freej* was an awareness of irony often absent in popular Arab comedy, which is generally of the slapstick variety. The show also tackles issues specific to Emiratis, such as local men marrying foreign women, even though local ladies can sometimes find it difficult to rustle up a husband. When the show did court controversy, it was religion that got it into trouble. During one episode, Um Hammas (think Homer Simpson in female form wearing traditional Emirati dress) donned a *niqab* over her *burqa* after having a quasi-religious epiphany. This attempt to lampoon religious hypocrisy was misinterpreted by some religious clerics as poking fun at Islam. Mohammed was forced to apologize publicly for any offense he may have given. Satire and irony are not yet comedic devices that everyone in Dubai appreciates.

But the success of *Freej* wasn't an accident. After returning from his studies in the US, Mohammed was fortunate to get an office job working for Dubai Media City – an attempt to show to the world that there is more to Dubai than baubles and trinkets, more to its business model than expensive horses and luxury resorts. Luckily for Mohammed, his boss accidently came across a comic he had sketched featuring his characters: wise-cracking local women in traditional dress. He was instructed to come up with a business plan and was given some money to make a pilot. The green light finally came after he secured some corporate sponsorship and a loan from the Sheikh Mohammed Enterprise Centre for Young Entrepreneurs.

From there, things began to accelerate. The storyboards and scripts were written and recorded in Mohammed's studio in Media City, while the animation work was done in India. Once the show hit the air, it rapidly became a success.

Freej was very much a product of the "cluster" model of economic development the emirate has fallen in love with. A quick glance at a city map reveals an embarrassment of these enterprises, be it Media City, Healthcare City, or Sports City. All it takes is four easy steps:

Step 1: Build and landscape a selection of office complexes stretching across a number of acres incorporating various-sized premises suitable for a wide range of different business enterprises.

Step 2: Stick a sign outside labeling the place Internet City, Chess City, or whatever other title you like. It shouldn't be complicated and subtlety is not encouraged. If at all possible, try to ensure that the word "city" is in the title. (It is worth noting that in Dubai, Knowledge only gets a Village while Horses get a City.)

Step 3: Announce to the world the creation of a pan-regional superhub of excellence for industries and support services related to the particular theme you have chosen – any remaining modesty to be checked in with security on arrival.

Step 4: Encourage, coax, or beg a host of global brands to set up shop in order to lend the whole enterprise an air of steely substance. Offer incentives to draw in the big brands; the herd will pile in afterwards and the rest of the units should sell themselves.

Prior to my visit, I had brushed up on this developmental model with the help of a local investment banker. He had explained the economic fundamentals underpinning Brand Dubai in general and the marketing of the city's various clusters in particular: "It's very simple. What is Knowledge Village or Healthcare City? Nothing, just desert! Pardon my French, but the authorities here just kiss ass, offer incentives, do whatever they have to in order to get some big name to set up in the first units they build, like Microsoft in Internet City. The first 10 percent of the units they almost give away. Then, when the big names are set up, all the other companies decide they have to be there too, especially the Arab companies. They want to piggyback on the reputation of the big international names. The big developers, the government, and the ruling family are all in it together. They make most of their money by selling the other 90 percent at really high prices."

Behind the hype, the developers of such projects have ambitious aims. While the oil sheikhs of the Gulf states may build motorways and skyscrapers with their petrodollars, at the first sign of a sniffle they fly to prestigious hospitals in the UK or the USA. Dubai wants to change that. The people behind Healthcare City (which is being developed in conjunction with Harvard Medical School) want to offer "world-class" services in the Middle East, but have the modesty to realize that they need outside help to do so. That said, the Mayo Clinic and Harley Street needn't worry about losing the aged Arab oil sheikh demographic just yet.

One area where the cluster model was certainly working was DMC. While I never doubted its powers of persuasion, the fact that the emirate was now home to some major global media players such as Reuters and CNN was a surprise. Dubai is not known as a bastion of free speech. When it comes to a free press, it has a lot in common with much of the developing world. Although a correspondent for BBC or CNN can always fly in and do an exposé, a local journalist may not feel free to do so. The solution to this potential pitfall lay with a seemingly inherent ability to have multiple (rather than simply double) standards. For example, there is a bipolar approach to the basic services offered to news organizations domiciled here. Websites that are normally blocked in Dubai can be accessed in these international clusters. In general, Dubai prefers to seduce rather than actively coerce. But as long as two rules apply, one for the local media and another for well-connected international players, there will always be some truth in the adage that "freedom of the press is limited to those who own one." Because the city entices international news organizations to base their regional offices in Dubai, there is another less polished axiom that may be more appropriate in this instance: it's better to have them on the inside pissing out, than on the outside pissing in.

If ownership equals influence, then the creation of a regional media center was an inevitable next step for Dubai and the other Gulf Arab states. After spending the twentieth century in the shadow of Egypt, Syria, and Iraq (traditionally the more influential Arab nations), the twenty-first looks set to be theirs. Traditionally, the Arabic news industry across the Gulf was the preserve of Egyptians, Sudanese, Lebanese, and Syrians born outside the Peninsula. During the first half of the twentieth century, Gulf societies were largely illiterate. In the television age, this balance of power has shifted and there has been a clear transmigration of influence. Although the top Arabic broadcasters and journalists still come from the more established journalistic and literary centers of Egypt and the Levant, some of the most popular Arabic news channels are now funded with Gulf money. The final stage in this process was to bring these stations home.

But Dubai Media City has its eyes set on more than mere news. The Arabic entertainment industry remains dominated by films and television programs produced in Egypt or Syria. The most-watched television shows across the Arab world each year are the month-long miniseries that air every evening during Ramadan. These television series range from Arabian sword-and-sandal epics depicting the battles of the early Muslim wars, to dramas dealing with touchy political issues, such as the overthrow of King Farouk of Egypt. And in recent years, there has been another addition to this pantheon of television shows: *Freej*.

Despite being a little rough around the edges, the local flavor of the show, with its snatched glimpses of a world often inaccessible to foreigners, makes it something special. Whereas Abu Dhabi had simply emptied a wheelbarrow of cash in front of the Guggenheim and the Louvre in its quest for a cultural identity, Dubai had taken a chance to nurture one of its own. And the more I thought about the *Mona Lisa with Burqa* hanging on the wall in his office, I wondered whether Mohammed was having a subtle joke at Abu Dhabi's expense.

Since its first series, *Freej* has grown considerably and has now been fully subsumed by Brand Dubai. Life-sized replicas of the characters greet visitors at the airport and DVD box sets are sold in the shops. This rapid trajectory notwithstanding, Mohammed was clearly still in shock at the most recent stage in the development of his pet project. His latest business partners were the moneymen behind Dubailand, the huge theme park planned for the desert just outside the city. They had recently announced plans to incorporate his *Freej* characters beside the other global brands planned for the project. "It's crazy! In a couple of years, we've gone from a doodle to a theme park," Mohammed said, creating a rather fitting motto for his home town.

8

Looking for a Lost Arabia

IT WAS TIME FOR A CHANGE. Dubai's already confining urban environment becomes even more claustrophobic in high summer. What is already a relatively small city by global standards becomes even more pocket-sized once you throw in a desperate need for air-conditioning. But along with a feeling of physical confinement, there was also a sense of mental constriction. I felt a lack of perspective from which to view the conversations and encounters that were part of my everyday life.

Although a broad picture of the city was forming in my mind, the portrait was still incomplete. I had seen Indians at prayer, Iranians at work, English at the gee-gees, Africans trying to strike it rich, and Pakistanis behind the wheel, but the local Arab people were proving harder to pin down. I had got a taste of the past talking to Mohammed about the old women in *Freej*, and I wanted some more. To understand the true significance of the journey Dubai had undergone, it was necessary get a sense of the distance that had been traveled. It was time to put some space between myself and what Tim Mackintosh-Smith called the "high-rise wadis of Arabia Concreta" and to sift through the primordial glop of Dubai's past.

While the emirate has a long maritime tradition, the ruling families of Dubai and Abu Dhabi share a common Bedouin lineage. The ancestors of both the Al Maktoum and the Al Nahyan families were desert people whose tribal heritage can be traced back to Liwa, a small oasis facing the expanse of the great Arabian desert near the border with Saudi Arabia. The past was readily available in the well-organized museums and cultural emporiums along-side the Creek, but I wanted a more visceral understanding of what had gone before. To do so, I had to broaden my horizons. Dubai and Arabia were proving elusive; the best I had managed so far was "Arabesque."

The road to Liwa takes you westward past the looming towers of the Dubai Marina project and the Bhopal chic of the Jebel Ali Industrial Area. In Thesiger's time, the land around Jebel Ali was still desert, at the outer fringes of the emirate. Since then, the city has expanded and engulfed everything before it in an outpouring of refineries, shopping malls, residential housing, and a massive container port. But once you put your foot down with any serious weight on Sheikh Zayed Road, the city quickly disappears in a puff of dust behind you. The eponymous Sheikh Zayed was the former ruler of Abu Dhabi and your transition from the emirate of Dubai to Abu Dhabi is modestly marked by a small hand-painted sign: a man and woman in traditional dress welcoming you with a wave. There is a clearer indication that you have moved from one princely domain to another, for the road immediately changes designation and becomes Sheikh Maktoum Bin Rashid Road, named after the former ruler of Dubai. Abu Dhabi has returned the compliment.

My map showed two avenues of approach. The first follows the main road, skirting around Abu Dhabi before passing through the towns of Tarif and Madinat Zayed. This second involves driving out into the desert along one of the straightest stretches of road in the world. I chose the more forsaken route. There is little sign of life until you reach the village of Shanayal, a blink-and-you-miss-it hamlet whose arid roads offer little enticement to passing traffic. Thus, *à la* Route 66, it takes a sizeable piece of hyperpituitarism to arrest the attention of passing motorists. An outsized replica of a Land Rover Defender lets you know that Shanayal is home to the Emirates National Auto Museum. The entrance to the museum is guarded by a modern-day Gryphon: a mutant Mercedes saloon kitted out with massive Big Foot tires. Inside, the centerpiece of the collection is an old American Dodge truck billed "The Largest Four-Wheel Drive in the World."

At this juncture, it is necessary to take a moment and qualify the position the 4x4 occupies in Arabia. Much more than just a form of transport, the 4x4 has replaced the camel as the most popular beast of burden in the deserts of the peninsula. As connoisseurs of both, there is little tolerance among local people for an inferior beast. Given the harsh desert conditions, endurance is the most prized asset. Thus, though the giant on display was American made, when it comes to tough desert driving in the twenty-first century the reliability of a Japanese model is preferred. The British journalist Robert Fisk recounts being driven to meet Osama Bin Laden in the mountains of Afghanistan, his driver reassuring him that "Toyota is good for *jihad*." The American travel writer Eric Hansen was the recipient of a spontaneous poem while walking in the mountains of Yemen, which placed Japanese engineering in some very lofty company:

> *I ask you merciful Allah, creator of heaven and earth,*
> *You who keep the moon travelling by night,*
> *and the sun by day,*
> *To protect Toyota Land Cruisers and foreign strangers*
> *Who climb to the mountaintops.*
> *And I conclude my prayer with a blessing on Mohammed,*
> *Who is honoured in all the lands.*

I spent some time ambling among the big yellow taxis that had taken a wrong turn somewhere in Manhattan and some gloriously dated sports cars, swapping stories with a Slovakian couple who were working in Abu Dhabi. Though refreshing some long-forgotten Czech expressions brought back pleasant memories, this wasn't the experience I was looking for. Avoiding the most direct route to Liwa hadn't been simply a matter of obduracy on my part. I had had my fill of multiculturalism. I was looking for a lost Arabia and didn't want to dillydally.

Beyond the museum, I felt that a threshold had been crossed. Surely, day-trippers would only make it as far as the museum before turning back. From here on things would be different – the real Arabia lay ahead! However, I hadn't got very far before my progress was interrupted by a solitary figure hitching a lift on the side of the road. I hesitated for a moment, then pulled over. Once the hitch-hiker was ensconced in the seat beside me, I got a quick biographical sketch, in a hodgepodge of English and Arabic, from my new traveling companion. Jalal was from Bangladesh. With the aid of my map, I learned that he was working as a carpenter in a small town a few miles before Liwa. After exhausting the basics, we fell into silence.

We drove on, beneath sandy overcast skies, past raspberry-ripple dunes that slip away into the horizon in an iron-oxide-induced symphony of vermilion tinged with ocher. Vast expanses of unforgiving sand rolled southward toward the Rub' al Khali. This is the name by which Arabs know the Empty Quarter, one of the world's fiercest deserts, which sprawls across the southern Arabian Peninsula for nearly half a million square miles, touching the UAE, Oman, Saudi Arabia, Qatar, and Yemen. It was to this harsh landscape that Thesiger was repeatedly drawn, making two epic crossings accompanied by a small group of native tribesmen. His lifelong goal achieved, Thesiger moved on to other isolated parts of the world, such as the marshlands of Iraq and the mountains of the Hindu Kush. Travel as he might amid some of the most spectacular scenery in the world, he never forgot *al Rimaal* (the Sands) and the *bedu* who accompanied him on his journeys. (Arab townspeople spoke of the Empty Quarter, among the *bedu* it was always the Sands.)

Sir Wilfred was just one in a long line of explorers for whom the deserts of Arabia have held a magnetic attraction. Influenced by Romantic poets and funded by imperial cash (the Anti-Locust Unit paid for Thesiger's travels in Arabia), generations of diplomats, historians, linguists, adventurers, and anthropologists have explored and lived among the people of the peninsula. Of those, many have penned odes to the landscapes and people they met, but Sir Wilfred's *Arabian Sands* is still one of the most widely fêted and read. Despite the pastoral origins of these infatuations, his book paints a far from glamorous picture of desert life. It depicts a harsh, bleak existence, yet one that offered an abundance of the quality he valued most: freedom.

The Arabian deserts have always had a fearsome reputation, a place where rapacious Bedouin were continually on the hunt for unsuspecting victims to pillage and plunder. This fear that even Arab urbanites had of the Bedouin was eloquently captured by Sir Charles Doughty (a truly one-of-a-kind Englishman) in a doorstop of a tome entitled *Travels in Arabia Deserta*. Those of a delicate disposition may prefer the abridged edition. On joining a *hajj* caravan departing Damascus for Mecca toward the end of the nineteenth century, Doughty was warned of the perils that lay ahead. In the eyes of his fellow travelers, the *bedu* were bandits who would gladly relieve a man of all his belongings and quite possibly his life: "Great is all townsmen's dread of the Beduw, as if they were the demons of this wild earth, ever ready to assail the Hajj passengers."

Not much had changed fifty years later, when Thesiger made his crossing of the Empty Quarter; security was still a constant concern. Even the tribesmen who accompanied him on his journey through the Sands were always on the lookout for raiders. The scarcity of even the most basic resources meant that the desert tribes were continually competing for access to water and food. The ever-present threat of thirst and starvation had created a culture where tribes regularly attacked each other just to survive. This raiding (and the killing and looting that went with it) were an intrinsic part of everyday existence. Bertram Thomas, another desert explorer and a contemporary of Thesiger, described how the *bedu* even used their own tribal law, rather than the Islamic *sharia*, to govern and regulate the inevitable disputes and blood feuds that arose from their combative lifestyle: "Disputes within the tribe are settled, as in general in tribal Arabia, by the *hakm al hauz*, a code of local sanctions, not the holy or Shara' law."

By the time Thesiger returned to the freshly sprouted steel and glass jungles of Dubai and Abu Dhabi in the 1970s, much had changed. And the old boy wasn't impressed. Soon after these states struck oil, a large amount of money was provided to settle the nomadic tribes. The result was one of the most radical and accelerated social shifts ever witnessed. In one generation, an entire way of life that had remained virtually unchanged for centuries disappeared. Thesiger had traveled through an Arabian twilight, a time when twentieth-century machinery was already unleashing irreparable changes. A letter written by a Political Agent during Thesiger's time contained a hint that the old way of life was no longer tenable:

On the 26th of May [three Manasir] raided two Bedouin encampments in Dubai territory. The men were away and the raiders succeeded in stealing from the women 8 camels, 2 rifles and their household effects. News reached Dubai that evening and the Shaikh of Dubai dispatched 30 men in two trucks to overtake the raiders. Next morning they engaged them at Bada' Khalifah in Abu Dhabi territory. Four of the Mansir were killed and the remaining two were captured and taken to Dubai... The two prisoners were well treated by the Shaikh of Dubai who gave them new clothes and daggers and sent them back to Abu Dhabi.

Modernity was infringing on the desert way of life with alacrity. That said, traditional hospitality was still in evidence. In Thesiger's view, the oil-fueled metempsychosis of the region constituted an "Arabian nightmare," as he feared that the local people would collectively disconnect from their past. He believed that a cultural death, rather than a rebirth, would be the ultimate bounty from the oil industry, drawing the Bedouin away from their nomadic lives in the desert to a sedentary existence near the oil fields and coastal towns.

A few kilometers before Liwa I dropped Jalal at home, a two-room Portacabin he shared with six other men. After I accepted his offer of a much-needed cup of tea, he guided me inside to meet his fellow workers. As it was Friday, they had only worked a few hours in the morning before prayers and they had the rest of the day off. They all had pictures to show me of wives and kids back home. Jalal explained that he had been in Abu Dhabi wiring money back home to his parents, the *raison d'être* of his current existence. I didn't stay long; my mind was elsewhere.

The weary wayfarer has a limited choice when it comes to accommodation in Liwa. The car park of the Liwa Rest House was deserted except for a solitary vehicle. An S in the sign outside was hanging on for dear life, ready to fall and impale the next passerby. Inside, the Indian receptionist couldn't conceal his shock at seeing a potential guest. Liwa in August is certainly not one of the world's prime tourist destinations. A quick inspection of the facilities revealed corridors covered in industrial tiles and drab rooms furnished with thin chipboard and uninspired bedding. I couldn't imagine any self-respecting locals from Dubai appreciating the sanatorium chic of the place and decided to look elsewhere. Nowadays, even desert camping trips come with satellite television, toilets, servants, and other conveniences. If locals were arriving in Liwa from Dubai to commune with their inner *bedu*, a few creature comforts would have to be in place.

Down the road, the swankier Liwa Hotel, perched on a hill with a broad view over the entire oasis, was clearly a better option for someone on the lookout for locals. The car park was full of expensive vehicles with Dubai license plates, and a brief conversation with a newly arrived guest as he locked up his Porsche Cayenne confirmed that this was the place for me. An Emirati from Dubai, he too was escaping the humidity and claustrophobia that afflict his home town each summer.

Inside, I discovered that the Liwa Hotel also had an interest in Thesiger and other British explorers of the Empty Quarter. A large map in the lobby detailed Sir Wilfred's several expeditions in the late 1940s. From a small brochure produced by the hotel, I learned that Liwa itself had its own Thesiger connection: he had passed through this very oasis on at least one occasion. The large map also highlighted the route taken by Bertram Thomas in 1931, the first foreigner to cross the Empty Quarter. He occupied himself on his travels (among other things) performing phrenological observations for the Royal Geographical Society by measuring the skulls of the natives he encountered. Thomas beat St. John Philby (father of the famous Cold War spy) to the plum of being the first Englishman across the Sands; Philby did so one year later. In *Arabian Sands*, Sir Wilfred paid tribute to those who went before him:

> *Thomas and Philby, whose names will always be remembered together in connexion with the crossing of the Empty Quarter, as the names of Amundsen and Scott will be associated with the South Pole.*

At the same time, Thesiger's competitive streak couldn't help but have a little dig at the efforts of those who beat him to the prize. Thomas crossed where "the dunes are small [and] wells... frequent," while Philby had benefited by having "obtained the Ibn Saud's permission and the king's far reaching authority."

Though Thesiger often wrote that it was solitude he sought when he explored such desolate places, this was not his only motivation. There was always the added appeal of being first and winning (in his own words) "distinction as a traveller." Even in the late 1940s, Liwa was still such a place:

> *It [Liwa] sounded very exciting, an oasis with palm groves and villages which extended for two days' camel journey. I knew no European had ever been there.*

Although not the first, or even the second, foreigner to cross the Empty Quarter, Thesiger is the explorer most associated with it. This a testament to the depth of his feelings for the *bedu* who accompanied him and his ability to transpose those emotions into words.

Although many more Europeans had visited Liwa since Thesiger's first foray, I also felt a sense of satisfaction with my own journey as I turned in for the night, even if I had used one of the infernal machines that Thesiger detested. His dislike of the motor car was intense. In *Arabian Sands*, he recalled taking a not insignificant amount of satisfaction when Philby (who at the time was on an errand for his boss, the King of Saudi Arabia) ran into some automotive difficulty while driving to meet him. Thesiger had incurred the wrath of the king for wandering through his territory without getting permission:

> *After dark we saw the lights of a car in the distance. Later we heard its engine racing and realized that it was stuck in the sand. Resenting all cars, especially in Arabia, I was rather pleased that it was in trouble... All my life I had hated machines... the speed and ease of mechanical transport must rob the world of all diversity... I would not myself have wished to cross the Empty Quarter in a car. Luckily this was impossible when I did my journeys, for to have done the journey on a camel when I could have done it in a car would have turned the venture into a stunt.*

The mosque was on the wrong side of the road, so I double checked the brochure the hotel had prepared for visitors such as myself, who were keen to walk in the footsteps of the great explorer:

> *Travel until you come to the Oasis of Qatuf, for those who have read* Arabian Sands, *this is where Sir Wilfred*

> *Thesiger camped during his visit to Liwa in 1947, look out*
> *for a mosque on the right, the wells he mentioned are*
> *located just beyond the old house there to your right.*

"Can't even get the bloody directions right," I whispered under my breath, unsure if I was referring to myself or the staff member at the hotel who had penned the information. The restraint was unnecessary. At midday in August, with the sun high overhead, the village of Qatuf was deserted. After a sound night's sleep, I had set myself a mission for the following morning: find the wells where Thesiger camped and soak up the atmosphere before retiring to my quarters for a siesta.

Driving out of Liwa, a road sign soon confirmed in both Arabic and English script that I had arrived in Maradha Qatuf (Qatuf Oasis), despite the fact that the only mosque in sight was decidedly on my left. I figured this was only a minor deviation and struck on regardless into the village. Even after his long crossing of the Sands, Thesiger's description of Qatuf was cool and rather detached:

> *We passed through the settlements of Qutuf and Dhaufir.*
> *Palms were planted along the salt flats, close under high*
> *steep-sided dunes, and in hollows in the sand. The groves*
> *were fenced in, and other fences were built along the dune-*
> *tops, to try and control the movement of The Sands, which*
> *in a few places had partly buried the trees...The Arabs here*
> *were Bani Yas. They lived in rectangular cabins made*
> *from palm fronds, built for the sake of coolness on the*
> *downs above the palm groves, two or three cabins being*
> *enclosed by a high fence and inhabited by one family.*

While known primarily as an explorer and a writer, Thesiger was also a prolific photographer. And one of his greatest legacies is the large collection of black-and-white photographs he left behind, which offer an insight into flickering cultures such as Iraq's Marsh Arabs. When I compared Thesiger's photographs of Liwa to what one can see today, the changes that forty-odd years had rent on the landscape were rather severe. However, the electricity pylons and paved roads of today could not completely overpower the impact of the surrounding scenery. Tall red dunes still tower over valleys thick with palm trees, crouching beneath these looming hills of sand. But in other parts of the oasis, fields of freshly cut hay trumpeted rather too loudly man's taming of the natural world. Yet just like in Thesiger's description, all this man-made development looked vulnerable. The encroaching desert had covered some of the lesser-used roads in sand. It was reassuring to know that without constant intervention, much of this human activity would eventually disappear under the desert's relentless advance.

The mosque was painted a brilliant white with touches of green on the sides. It was in much better condition than the houses nearby, which were all ramshackle one-story affairs. A road sign indicated there were some farms over a nearby hill. I guessed the best place for a farm would be near a well and drove on. The only problem was the firmness of the track. Reassuringly, tire tracks ran over the top and the surface appeared solid. I soon crested the hill, but no wells came into view. I decided to turn back. Halfway through a three-point turn, the car came to a grinding halt. I pressed hard on the accelerator but to no avail, the tires merely sank further into the sand. I was stuck. A quick inspection from outside revealed only one course of action, but my initial attempts to dig my way out with a piece of wood from a nearby rubbish pile proved fruitless. Though I was out of the car for only five minutes, the sun was already making me light-headed. My decision to embark on a desert pilgrimage at the beginning of August was beginning to seem more idiotic by the minute. Help was needed.

Possibly due to my Catholic upbringing, I turned to religion. Surely a passing parishioner frequenting the mosque would feel compelled (out of guilt at least) to assist a stranger in distress? So I downed my tools and began to march across the sand. After a few yards, the surface underfoot grew softer and with each step, sand began to seep inside my sandals. While open-toed Italian leather may cut a dash in a five-star resort, they certainly weren't the best choice for this kind of terrain. Within a few seconds, a burning sensation erupted on the soles of my feet. The air is not the only thing that gets up to 50 degrees Celsius in summer. "Jesus Christ!" I shouted in the direction of the mosque and the thankfully deserted village, hopping across the sand and moving from one foot to another, like a hapless victim in a Tom and Jerry cartoon. By the time I made it back to the safety of the asphalt, I was out of breath, dizzy, and more than a little red-faced. Standing there on the road, shaking off the dust, my car immobilized, I sensed the ghost of Sir Wilfred having another guffaw at the limitations of the motor car and the modern world.

Thankfully, in the shadow of the mosque salvation was at hand. Not in the form of a religious epiphany from on high, but a Toyota Landcruiser driven by an Emirati man from the local municipality. "*Ana ghabi!*" (I am stupid!) I exclaimed once inside, pointing to my car stuck in the sand. My own personal savior politely rejected this hypothesis, despite a host of rather damning supporting evidence. We drove around the village until he stopped outside one of the simple brick houses and tooted the horn a few times. A rather disheveled-looking man appeared, obviously disturbed from an afternoon nap. They exchanged a few words and the man disappeared indoors again, only to re-emerge a minute later with a towrope. Throughout this interchange, the Emirati addressed the man with the rope simply as Baluchi. It became clear that while the Emirati was providing the logistics, Mr. Baluchi would be supplying whatever elbow grease was required. A few minutes later, all was right with the world and I was back on the road. From then on, I resolved to stick to hard surfaces and bugger the wells.

Liwa's premier attraction proved much more accessible. Moreeb Hill is a 287-meter-high sand dune reached by a stretch of firm, unyielding tarmac. The road undulates through wide salt flats and sculpted dunes, with rivulets of sand sliding intricately to the ground. Along the way, the ground is pockmarked by plucky green shrubs in a remarkable display of nature's resilience. The interplay of all this color and light was hypnotic.

Though one might expect the modern world to genuflect in front of all this uncultivated beauty, this is not necessarily the case. For Moreeb Hill plays host each year to a monster dune-bashing derby, when thousands gather to watch young petrolheads from across the Gulf go head to head with the mother of all dunes in high-powered four-wheel drives and on supercharged motorbikes. Drag racing Arabian style! That midsummer afternoon the venue was empty, but the infrastructure for these contests was still there. Along with the floodlights, Portacabins, and sponsors' advertising hoardings, there was even a helipad for incoming dignitaries. Closing my eyes, I tried to picture the scene each spring: scores of pumped up *shebab* blasting their way up the dune in an epic contest of machine versus nature. Though I hesitate to put words in the mouths of the dearly departed, it is safe to assume that Sir Wilfred wouldn't have been the most enthusiastic supporter of the event.

I drove back to Liwa in a heat-induced daze. Scattered around the outskirts of the town were a number of lonely looking *baqalas* (grocery stores), manned by a succession of increasingly lonely Indian men. One shopkeeper told me he had been here for twenty-five years. "When I first came here, there were only camels, no cars, no roads," he said. Another, younger man seemed to despair at where he had ended up. "What is here?" he asked, raising his hands to heaven.

The town of Liwa is a sleepy but not unpleasant gathering. Its population comprises a resident and seasonal Emirati population, along with an army of Asians who take care of all the physical work that goes along with maintaining an oasis. The streets have footpaths and paved roads and there are a number of old-style American strip malls. The shops have names such as Flying Saucer Agricultural Materials or Perfect Climate Grocery, though I don't know which of the two sounds the more preposterous.

In the mood to forage on some local fodder, I kept my eyes open for a restaurant as I drove through. When a red-checked *gutra* and a white *kandura* in a window caught my eye, I pulled over, hoping to join some local men dining on the traditional Bedouin favorite of lamb and rice. Once inside, far from being a scion of local *bedu* stock, the man in the *gutra* turned out to be from Bangladesh: the *imam* of the local mosque. I scoured the menu, but my plan to end my day with some Bedouin food didn't work out. After a quick chat with the cook, I ordered the dal fry instead.

As I ate, I learned that the entire clientele hailed from Bangladesh; they were wiling away the evening watching the news beamed from home by satellite television. The lead story was a flood that had just struck their homeland. The storm waters had killed thousands and left even more homeless and destitute. Everyone was glued to the images that flashed by on the screen: flimsy houses built on stilts with high waters running beneath. One image in particular stayed with me. A woman was crouched in a boat with two naked children sitting alongside her, their bellies swollen from malnutrition, gliding though a flood of dank, filthy water. I wondered where the father was. It was only later I realized that there was a distinct possibility he could have been sitting beside me.

The following morning I rose early and made my way back to Qatuf, determined to have a final crack at finding the wells before the long drive back to Dubai. Even though I followed the instructions more carefully the second time around, the result was still the same. The mosque from the previous day's outing was still on the wrong side of the road, stubbornly refusing to cooperate. A careful exploration of the laneways on either side also proved fruitless; there were no wells to be seen. I was disappointed. Finding the wells had become important for me, as the continual pursuit of water (along with its scarceness) is a recurring theme throughout *Arabian Sands*, and even bothered Sir Wilfred's subconscious as he slept:

> *But my thirst troubled me the most... Even when I was asleep I dreamt of racing streams of icecold water... I worried about the water which I had watched dripping on the sand... Then I worried about whether we had tied the mouth of the skin properly when we had last drawn water... It was easy to banish these thoughts in daylight, less easy in the lonely darkness.*

Even after a well was found, the reality was far from his dreams. They were often filled in with sand and had to be dug out before water could be drawn. And instead of ice-cold springs, they often only yielded barely drinkable brackish water. One of Sir Wilfred's photographs captures this moment perfectly: three of his Bedouin companions stripped to the waist covered in sand, offering water in leather skins to the camels gathered around them.

Somewhat disheartened that the wells had eluded me, I drove a kilometer or two out of Mahdhar Qatuf until I passed a sign heralding the next collection of palm trees as Mahdhar Wafd. However, a small mosque soon appeared and a quick look at my directions revealed it was on the right side of the road! A *boreen* (I have yet to come across a more pleasant way to describe a small country lane than this Irish word) tailed off the main road toward some palm trees huddled beneath an imposing wall of red dunes. Once on foot, there was another encouraging sign – the old house mentioned in my brochure.

I thought I was alone, but as I neared a grove of date palms, voices began to drift out from behind the trees. Walking inside, I came across three men sitting on the ground in the shade. They were sorting out mounds of caramel- and port-colored dates for shipment to the *souks* of Dubai, Abu Dhabi, and beyond. Bare-chested and dressed in sarongs or pyjama-like trousers, they had the burnished complexion of the Bangladeshi men I had dined with the previous night.

"Water?" I asked obtusely, pointing to the ground. One of the men understood immediately and beckoned me forward. We walked farther into the shaded palm grove until he stopped and pointed downwards. There, jutting a few inches out of the ground, was an eight-inch-wide yellow plastic pipe. A few feet further along, a metal pipe with two rubber hoses branched out at ground level. Here were the famed wells of Liwa! While I hadn't been expecting living and breathing figures straight from the pages of *Arabian Sands*, it was still rather anticlimactic.

Despite the time I had invested in my search for the wells, I was keen to get going. The usual mishmash of Arabic and English I often employed in such situations (I didn't speak Bengali, their mother tongue) wasn't working very well. There was another invite for tea, but I declined and said my goodbyes, in no mood to sit through another stilted conversation on the same topics of country, employ-ment, and family. From the carpenter hitching on the side of the road to the *imam* in the restaurant, and these farmhands working the wells, the Empty Quarter had morphed into an outpost of Bangladesh.

Thesiger had insisted that it was the companionship of the *bedu* that had given him the greatest joy in his traveling life. "Without it these journeys would have been a meaning-less penance," he wrote. The men Thesiger admired so much had braved the harshest of elements with fortitude, and their life offered little in the way of comfort or material posses-sions. These are the men you see in the black-and-white pho-tographs in *Arabian Sands*, bare-chested and hauling water from the wells while their camels wait stoically for a drink. Today the picture has changed, but it has also stayed the same. There are still tough customers working the wells around the Empty Quarter, but they now hail from far across the Arabian Sea. What did all this desert mean to these men: a paycheck, a penance, a purgatory? I decided there and then that if I wanted to commune with the world Thesiger had traveled through, it was time to start learning Bengali.

On the road back to Dubai, I stopped at a cemetery on the outskirts of town. Like much of my time spent outdoors around Liwa, I had the place to myself, not another living soul in sight. This sense of isolation was further increased by a perimeter wall lined with trees secluding the cemetery from the outside world. In much of the Arabian Peninsula, it is customary to put some distance between the living and the dead and excessive lamentation for the deceased is not encouraged. The theory is simple: the living should worry about themselves and Allah will take care of the departed. At least this is the Sunni way in much of the Gulf, an approach to mortality that strikes some foreigners as rather cold and heartless. This attitude is manifested by the absence of ornate (or in some cases even marked) head-stones in many cemeteries. When King Fahad of Saudi Arabia passed away, he was buried without as much as a tombstone, though such modesty was in contrast to the opulence that marked his days among the living.

But even here, time refused to stand still and the grad-ual evolution/amelioration/disintegration (delete as appropriate) of the culture Sir Wilfred had admired could be witnessed at first hand. Interspersed between the older unmarked graves were a handful of recently entombed res-idents, whose passing had been marked in more definitive terms with names and dates etched in Arabic calligraphy on grey marble. This naming of the dead was a twenty-first-century innovation; *bidah* is the theological term. Traditionalists can have a hard time reconciling such changes with what they see as a sundering of the estab-lished order. They fear that any alteration to the practice of Islam will ultimately be the undoing of their way of life, a loose thread that will unravel everything.

The earliest year I found on any of the marked graves was 2001, revealing how all traditions and beliefs, no mat-ter how deeply entrenched or fervently held, are suscepti-ble to time's relentless abrasion. And as I stood there in the late afternoon sun, a number of questions arose. Is it ever possible truly to understand what has gone before? Is it possible to understand the future by digging around in the detritus of the past? Is it even possible that some of the people Thesiger greeted, as his party trudged slowly through Liwa all those years ago, ended up buried here many years later, silent witnesses to this changing world?

9
City of Gold

I HAD NEVER BEEN to a Bangladeshi nightclub before. Beneath a low stage festooned brightly from above with unseasonal Christmas decorations, a floor show of nine young women dressed in saris moved unenthusiastically in time with the music. Out in front, a tall male singer worked the floor, singing along to backing tracks preened from an assortment of Hindi and Bengali films. Compared to the hotel bar on the ground floor, where a selection of Gulf Arabs in white robes and gold-adorned African men were carousing with a transglobal selection of working girls, Brahmaputra Nights was, on the surface at least, the height of good taste. Just in case the clientele lost the run of themselves, a wiry Yemeni from the Hadhramut Mountains was deployed as a bouncer near the entrance. He was dressed traditionally, in a faded double-breasted jacket worn over a long white robe, but without the customary dagger that would undoubtedly have been sported were he pacing the streets of Shebam. All in all, it was a cabaret-cum-floorshow you could bring your grandmother to without fear of embarrassment – unlike many of Dubai's other nocturnal establishments.

After the open spaces around Liwa, returning to the urban jungle of Baniyas Square was disconcerting. In comparison to the unending expanse of the Empty Quarter, the city's busy horizon of skyscrapers spoke more of limits and constriction. My trip away had been frustrating but cathartic and I had finally given up worrying about what constituted the "real" Dubai. Authenticity is what you find, not what you expect.

The stares that greeted my entrance to the nightclub indicated that the regulars weren't totally comfortable with Dubai's global village aspirations. Despite the much-vaunted statistic that more than 150 nationalities live in Dubai, people tend to stick with their own. In this hotel alone, there was also a Russian and an Iranian nightclub, while the city's many South Indian hot spots were not in the least concerned about losing customers to establishments such as the Jet Set African Nightclub. Unlike the Irish pubs and Italian restaurants, these establishments are not targeting a broad demographic; they are places of refuge for men who can spend years away from home. Whether it is through a song they liked as a child or the smile of a woman reminding them of someone they knew back home, these men here just wanted to be teleported back to Bangladesh for a few hours. Out of the city's multilayered immigrant communities, Bangladeshis are definite contenders for Dubai's most inglorious superlative: Most Wretched Expat Population. Despite stiff competition for the crown from Baluchis, Indians, and Pakistanis, they make up a significant chunk of the poorest and most destitute inhabitants.

After taking a seat with a good view of the stage, I fell into a halting conversation with a man at the next table. With the help of his ID card, Jangil explained that he worked as a welder for a local construction company. From a little village outside the Bangladeshi capital of Dakka, he had lived in Dubai for nearly ten years. The singer bursting into song impeded our conversation, so we sat back and enjoyed the show.

A rainbow of colors sprang from the bench at the back of the stage as the dancers launched into a rather sedate Bollywood routine, which involved much flexing of the elbow and wrist. Patrolling the floor was a master of ceremonies, who eventually walked up to my table and said something in my ear. The singer's loud rendition of old Hindi favorites (I'm pretty sure Mukesh Chand Mathur got an airing) made it difficult to hear, so Jangil leaned over and explained what was going on. For 50 dirhams (around US$15), one of the girls would dedicate her dance especially to me. I had a hard time grasping the concept until a customer at another table beckoned the MC toward him and handed over some cash. Once the message and the money had been conveyed to the girl in question, the chorus line took a step back. The girl continued to dance exactly as before, only now she was looking the man directly in the eye. If this is what constitutes a Bangladeshi lap dance, it wouldn't have caused much of a stir in an Amish village hall.

Now that things had been set in motion, other customers joined in. At the table to my right, a rather rotund man was writing something on a scrap of paper, which (along with 50 dirhams) he passed to the MC. "What's in the note?" I asked Jangil. "They say, 'I love you, you are beautiful,' something like this," he answered. I watched more closely this time. Once the money had been passed to the object of his affections, a girl in a black and gold sari took a step forward and danced for the big fella, continuing to hold his gaze as she moved demurely in time with the music. After his dance was finished, the man (who like the dancers was also from Bangladesh) turned around. Clearly very inebriated, he was in the mood to chat. He wanted to get something off his chest. "The municipality fined me 15,000 dirhams (around US$4,000) today," he lamented, crying a river into his beer. To explain why, he leaned in close and bellowed out the details of his misfortune at an eardrum-bursting volume, as all drinkers do, regardless of nationality.

The big fella's business was bed space. This is a system whereby the poorest workers in the city sleep six or eight to a room, literally paying rent for the space occupied by a single bed. He had a simple business model: he rented large, run-down villas and partitioned them into smaller rooms, before subletting as many bed spaces as he could squeeze in. The most extreme form of this activity is what submariners in the Royal Navy call "hot-bedding," when two people share the same bed that they use on alternate shifts. Advertisements offering bed space are common across the city, but even this lowest end of the housing market is delineated in terms of ethnicity, religion, and social class. The following is indicative of the signs you find pasted on walls in Deira and Bur Dubai:

> *One bed space for Tamil Muslim*
> *Executive bachelor*
> *Near Naif Park*
> *Single cot*
> *460 per month + DEWA [electricity and water]*

Most bed spaces violate planning regulations, yet an incalculable number of immigrants depend on them for accommodation. Reports of accidents occasionally creep into the media, usually when there is a fire; given the overcrowded conditions, tenants sometimes overload the wiring.

From his demeanor, the big fella clearly felt he had been unlucky to be fined. In much of the Gulf the concept of what is illegal can be very flexible, even in Dubai, which has a reputation for following the rules. Illegal renting practices may be ignored for years until a headline-grabbing event leads to a public outcry. For example, many nightclub dancers are locked in their apartments during daylight hours, supposedly for their own "safety." The story only breaks when disaster strikes, such as a fire in an apartment building that incinerates two unfortunates. The press calls for a clampdown while ministers and senior officials are "shocked" (think Claude Rains in *Casablanca*) that such illegality is going on. They promise that all violators will be severely dealt with. A crackdown ensues, premises are raided, and fines are levied. But after a few weeks, everything quietly reverts to normal. After all, if someone with connections owns the building, it's not going to sit idle for long. Though I could understand his pain, it was hard to feel sorry for the big fella. If he could afford a 15,000 dirham fine, he must be doing all right.

His story exemplifies how the one-dimensional image of Asian poverty in Dubai – wealthy Arabs lording it over downtrodden immigrants from the Asian subcontinent – is clearly a gross oversimplification. The most proficient exploiters of any race are those who know them best. This was a lesson I learned one night after landing at Dubai International Airport, where, outside the arrivals hall, I came across a group of close to a hundred young men. Dubai virgins, they were "fresh off the boat" from Bangladesh. This would be their first time away from home and not one of them could have weighed more than 50 kilos. Their skinny torsos failed to provide enough meat to flesh out the matching blue-and-pink t-shirts they had been issued by the "manpower" company that had brought them here. Huddled close together, their eyes darted back and forth nervously as they took in their new surroundings, clearly unsure what was going to happen next. Passing through the airport terminal, they would have seen shiny advertisements for glistening new housing developments, promising buyers the "ultimate lifestyle" if they relocated to Dubai.

The leader of the group was an older man from the subcontinent dressed in a pressed shirt and slacks, no doubt a middle manager with the recruitment firm that had brought them to Dubai. Of an age to be a father to any of those young men, he was trying to herd his charges into something resembling an orderly line. Constrained by a lack of space, one young man at the front was pushed forward. The older man immediately grabbed him by the shirt and violently pushed him back, following this with a torrent of abuse and curses. Welcome to Dubai.

I stepped in and gave him a piece of my mind. The older man quickly broke into an obsequious smile and raised his hands to heaven, as if to say, "How else can I deal with these people?" Just then another man leaving the airport joined in and harangued him in Hindi. I left them at it and jumped into a nearby taxi. As we drove off, it was clear that the driver had seen it all before: "These people get paid nothing. Here, construction laborers are not worth anything but shit."

When last orders were called at the nightclub, Jangil and I exchanged numbers and agreed to meet a few days later. This time we met somewhere quieter. We toured around Baniyas Square and the *souks* of Deira, and ate *shwarma* and ice cream while I learned a little more about his life in Dubai. He lived in a labor camp in the suburbs, a vast, sprawling conurbation of bachelors. These are the men who provide the elbow grease that keeps Dubai ticking along. Compared to some of his other countrymen, Jangil wasn't doing that badly. He was earning about 1,400 dirhams (nearly US$400) a month and his accommodation was provided by his employer. Breaking this chain generally involved disappearing into Dubai's black economy. Anyway, the salary he received meant he could send some money home to his parents every month (to a country where millions survive on US$30–60 a month), while also putting a little aside to get married and raise a family some day. There was even a little left over to go to a nightclub every so often and listen to some songs that reminded him of home. Maybe something even remained to write a note to one of the girls who may have caught his eye, telling her "I love you."

The poster from the Bangladeshi tourist board with the optimistic logo was hanging proudly on a wall in the Bangladeshi consulate:

Visit Bangladesh
Before tourists come

The slogan was accompanied by a photograph of a man dressed in a blue-checked sarong and a thin white vest. This poster child for the country's tourist ambitions carried a large bushel of wheat on his head – a picture of pastoral bliss. It is young men like this, the sons of poor Bangladeshi farmers, who fill the ranks of Dubai's bloated construction and cleaning industries. The path that takes men like Jangil from a flooded field in Bangladesh to the dusty deserts of Dubai is well trodden. Father either borrows the cash or sells some land to finance the trip. The recruitment agency in Bangladesh charges a fee of US$2,000–3,000 for the flight, the visa, and a job in Dubai. This is despite the fact that under UAE law it is illegal for prospective employees to pay these expenses; the fees should be borne by the employer. Larger, more respectable companies often bypass such regulations by using subcontractors to keep any dirty work at arm's length.

On arrival, the men's passports are taken by their employer. However, the salary is often lower than what was promised and/or there is a long list of charges to be paid to the recruiter, which are deducted from their salary over several months. Sometimes, the salary doesn't come at all or is delayed. This is a more common occurrence for those working for a small-time subcontractor with cash-flow issues.

Many men spend the first few years paying back the loan they took out to get to Dubai in the first place before they can save any money. For some, this situation is simply not feasible, so they abandon their employer and seek illegal work elsewhere. Their visa and residency papers are then canceled by the recruiter. They are now illegal absconders in a foreign country without a passport. Even if they want to, they cannot leave. This is a path that eventually leads back to their consulate in search of help.

The issue of Asian workers receiving minimal salaries inevitably crops up in any examination of Dubai. These lowly paid workers – from the triptych of Pakistan, India, and Bangladesh – are easily identifiable from the rest of the population lined up by the score in their blue or yellow overalls. While there are hundreds of thousands of such workers, this is not a topic that the local authorities are quick to embrace. As such, it is diplomats from these three South Asian countries who are often the most informed about the issue; the only difficultly is to getting them to talk candidly.

A previous meeting with the Bangladeshi ambassador in Kuwait regarding the exploitation of his countrymen had been an affable but ultimately fruitless affair. Successful diplomats spend their lives perfecting the art of speaking at length while often saying little of substance. You don't rise to the rank of ambassador by talking frankly, at least not on the record. So after stumbling across the Bangladeshi consulate in the back streets of

Deira, I adopted a different approach and decided against requesting a formal interview. Instead, I wandered in and assumed the role of a holidaymaker in need of a visa. Once in the office of the correct official, I took a seat and waited my turn. It was busy. The diplomat offered to deal with my enquiry first but I deferred, content to sit and watch. Although of ordinary height, he was still a good eight inches taller than the five-foot-nothings gathered around his desk, who all wore the same hangdog expression. The powers that be had recently declared an amnesty for all illegal workers and the deadline for applications was fast approaching. The men were here looking for an outpass: a no-questions-asked, get-out-of-jail-free card, as long as they were willing to leave the country. The amnesty had received praise from some quarters as an enlightened approach to a difficult problem, but essentially it was a laxative designed to purge the bowels of Dubai's unregulated labor market.

No matter how hard the city tries, however, there are still illegal workers who do not want to go home. During the day they are a shadowy force, mingling with the hundreds of thousands of legal Asian workers in the city. It's only at night that the streets belong to them. While Dubai is by no means a 24-hour city, it is possible to sit down to a good meal at any time of the day. And even at 4 a.m., the Lebanese restaurant where I passed a few nocturnal hours one night was still busy. The table next to me was occupied by well-fed Asian men. Well groomed and sharply dressed, they had the full range of accessories the modern man needs to signify his status in society. Hefty designer watches, gold jewelry, the latest mobile phones, and suitably chunky car keys all indicated achievement, while dinner consisted of large plates of grilled meat. Success, in any man's language.

Just across the road, only a few meters away, there's a story with a different ending. Hidden from the passing eye in a little park running through the center of Al Muteena Street you can find men for whom things are not so rosy. These are the flotsam and jetsam of the Dubai dream, the sweepings of the global economy.

It's while walking through the park that the noctilucent side of the city reveals itself. Within the first few yards I see about eight men sleeping rough, asleep on benches or lying motionless on the ground. After walking another fifty yards the number rises rapidly, from twenty to thirty to forty. Some of them are bare-chested and dressed only in sarongs. The lucky ones have pieces of cardboard beneath them as makeshift mattresses; otherwise they sleep on grass or concrete. Continuing down the street, the count rises: fifty... sixty... seventy... eighty... ninety. One man has an arm and a leg thrown over a park bench, the way a child nuzzles up to a cuddly toy or a lover nestles up close to their beloved. I'm still only two thirds of the way down the street when my count passes a hundred. Another man is asleep on the cement, avoiding an unwelcome sprinkler spraying water on an otherwise coveted patch of grass. Further along, others sit in groups on the concrete, spending the night playing gin rummy. By the end of this one street, my count has reached 174 homeless men. I walk back up the street again, perplexed and looking for explanations.

One man stands out, dressed in a suit and talking to a group of men gathered around a bench. I don't feel like finessing the situation. I walk straight up to him and the questions pour out: "Where are all these guys from? Why are they sleeping here? Are they waiting for an outpass?"

He enlightens me: "No. They are all working here in Dubai, mainly from India. But their salary is very small, only about 1,200 dirhams (US$325) a month. A bed space is about 600 a month, food maybe 400, so if they take a place to sleep, they can't save any money." Most of the men had absconded from their employers, generally for nonpayment or underpayment of salaries. (A taxi driver once told me that the most notorious nonpayers were local, Indian, and Pakistani companies. He insisted that European companies didn't behave like this. I'd like to believe him.) "The construction guys who live in the labor camps are alright, they have company accommodation, bathrooms, kitchens, and showers," the suit added. The men sitting beside him nodded enviously in agreement.

I was shocked. Amnesty International had documented the poor working and living conditions of construction workers in the labor camps outside the city. I had assumed these were the people who had it the worst, that they were the ones eking out an existence at the bottom of the barrel. I was mistaken. It seems if you scrape hard enough, there's always going to be another layer of destitution underneath.

🌴

Months later, I was sitting in a room in the sprawling labor camp of Sonapur. This suburb-cum-shantytown, which has grown up on the outskirts of the city, is home to thousands of South Asian bricklayers, carpenters, welders, and machinery operators. The room measured about 12 feet by 9 and was home to three bunk beds and six men, all from the southern Indian state of Kerala. For a six-day working week, they receive a monthly salary that hovers around US$175, even though the average per capita income in the UAE is US$2,106 a month – a difference of 1,200 percent.

In Hindi, the word Sonapur means "city of gold." The camp houses the men who built the dream palaces of the imagination such as Burj Dubai or the Palm Jumeirah, yet the authorities are loath to acknowledge their existence. The powers that be aren't afraid to put projects not yet built on the official city map, yet you could scour every map in the emirate and find no trace of Sonapur, vital and thriving though it may be. As Dubai has grown, new labor camps have opened up elsewhere to cope with the over-spill, but Sonapur remains the original of the species.

My intention had been to hold off visiting Sonapur until the end of my time in Dubai. This was to avoid any potential complications that might arise from rummaging through the city's dirty laundry. The authorities are highly sensitive on this matter. When covering the opening of a new hotel, journalists are welcomed with open arms and no expense is spared to show them the best Dubai has to offer. It's only if the reporter veers off message that the authorities express their displeasure. A documentary filmmaker investigating the city's prostitution industry claimed that her hotel room was mysteriously "burgled" during her stay, and that the police also tried to confiscate some of her video footage; another researcher on a prestigious scholarship was detained by the police and had the hard drive taken from his computer. Regarding Sonapur in particular, a further researcher described dodging security guards while sneaking into a camp to investigate the living conditions there.

The chance to see Sonapur for myself came about one afternoon while my mind was elsewhere. I was touring the outlying suburbs of Dubai, looking for the suburban sanctuaries to which the local population were retreating in ever-increasing numbers. Many locals were choosing to live in large family housing compounds in order to escape the development that has left many of the emirate's older generation strangers in their own country. Driving past a line of newly built villas in the Mizhar area, I stopped to give a lift to four men hitching on the side of the road. Once we had introduced ourselves and established the twin towers of nationality (India) and occupation (construction workers), they got comfortable and chatted among themselves. I paid little attention, lost in my own daydreams. It was only when the word "Sonapur" popped up in their conversation that I started to listen intently. This was an opportunity too good to turn down; as I had read somewhere, a chance encounter is better than a thousand appointments. Although my passengers were happy to be dropped off by the side of the road, I insisted on driving them all the way to their front door.

We turned our backs on the new houses sprouting to life behind us and veered off the road into the sand. We drove across a well-worn track that had already been pounded into a semi-solid state by other traffic. When we arrived at a metal gate, a security guard appeared. He compared who was behind the wheel with the four other men in the car, and a confused look spread across his face. But all it took was a wave and a smile and it was open sesame. He unlatched the gate and beckoned us through.

Inside, it was the sheer size of the place that surprised me most. There were scores of different camps, varying in design from ramshackle assemblages of breezeblock to modern three-story prefabricated structures. Each had its own team of security guards, and a sign outside one declared "No visitors allowed inside camp." My passengers pointed toward an older-looking building with a corrugated iron gate and indicated that they were home. As they got out of the car an invitation inside wasn't forthcoming, so I asked for some water.

Behind the gate there was an open courtyard surrounded by a single-story building, which contained their sleeping quarters, a kitchen, and a bathroom. The bed-room had bunk beds and lockers, while a television in one corner played a film in their native tongue of Malayalam. The religious diversity for which Kerala is noted was also in evidence: Jesus Christ adorned the walls next to intricate Islamic inscriptions. We sat on the beds as tea was pre-pared. Others joined us, freshly showered and dressed in the brightly coloured sarongs or *lungis* of southern India.

Once my tea was done I didn't loiter, not wanting to get anyone into trouble. Given the oversupply of cheap labor across the Indian subcontinent, those men could ill afford to lose their jobs. Workers who break Dubai's golden rule – Be Happy in Your Work – receive harsh treatment from the authorities if they deviate from this unwritten covenant. When construction workers rioted on the site of Burj Dubai over pay and conditions, a number of the ring-leaders (as they were dubbed) were arrested and subse-quently deported. So I said my goodbyes and left.

It was only as I drove around looking for a way out that I realized that Sonapur is not a hermetically sealed environ-ment. It is in fact a fully functioning suburb of the city, complete with restaurants, internet cafés, barber shops, medical clinics, and even a bus station. I could have taken a bus straight here, if only it had been marked on a map. Farther on, a line of shops had an ATM, a grocery shop, and a mobile phone dealer. And right in the middle of this cartographically challenged conglomeration of dust, sweat, and breezeblock was a gold merchant: bangles, rings, ear-rings, and necklaces glittering bright and luminous through the shop window. It made sense. Gold is the rea-son so many Asians come to Dubai in the first place, so they can afford the customary gold wedding sets required in the subcontinent, either for themselves or a family member. A poster in the window exhorted passersby to

"Fan Your Golden Dreams – one kilo of gold to be won every day during the Dubai Shopping Festival!" Momentarily, a depressing cycle of gold-induced indenture ran through my head. Men come here to earn the money they need to wed and have children (or to pay dowries for their daughters), but would their own children and grand-children grow up chasing the same gold for the same reasons? Or would the money sent back to Dakka, Cochin, and Karachi be enough to break this cycle?

Such thoughts, though potent at the time, ultimately prove to be ephemeral and pass as quickly as they come. Living in Dubai can have a distorting effect on your sensibilities. This kingdom of bling not only alters your perception regarding an acceptable level of wealth, such as what kind of car you want to drive or what manner of hotel you find acceptable; you also become acclimatized to the unavoidable corollary of such wealth. As I looked around at the long lines of prefabricated huts with lines of freshly washed blue overalls hanging in the breeze, and as a man squatted down to relieve himself in a makeshift open sewer, I also realized that living in this part of the world distorts one's idea of an acceptable level of poverty.

10

Shine On You Crazy Diamond

THE YOUNG MUSCOVITE WAS SELLING SHANGRI-LA by the square meter. Every shopping mall had the same set-up: a phalanx of kiosks and well-preened sales teams offering the chance to buy a little piece of the Dubai dream. His sales pitch was breezy and effervescent. He castigated his countrymen's lack of subtlety when it came to buying property: "Russian customers are stupid. They just throw their money around. They say, 'I don't care about the price! Just give me the best.'" While this seemed to reinforce the modern stereotype of Russians as arrivistes with more money than sense, he then started praising the investment acumen of European investors. This was a classic sales technique: massaging your ego and making you feel more intelligent than the next guy, but only if you buy. I imagined he had a different spiel for his Russian clients: "I won't bother showing you this piece-of-shit apartment. I only show that to those poor old Brits who don't have a pot to piss in. You look like a man who needs a villa..." By his reckoning, if I bought a property before breakfast, it would double in value by the time I sat down to lunch.

In the past, western expats came to Arabia simply for the money. In the 1970s, even though expat salaries were high, it still qualified as a "hardship" posting. Furthermore, British companies operating in the Gulf were not necessarily as picky about potential employees as they might have been at home. So the Gulf developed a reputation as a sanctuary for those with a past peppered with peccadilloes. As one rather jaded Englishman remarked, "Working in the Gulf, it's all rather Foreign Legion stuff, never ask a chap about his past." Nevertheless, it would be unfair to label all the westerners in Dubai as "pampered mercenaries... living in a social world that recalls the lost splendour of gin-and-tonics at Raffles and white mischief in Simla's bungalows" (in the words of Mike Davis, an immensely readable yet occasionally hyperbolic American academic). Hailing from countries as far apart as the US, South Africa, Zimbabwe, New Zealand, France, and Germany, most "westerners" simply aren't paid enough (except for the lawyers of course) to earn the moniker of mercenaries. White flesh is abundant in Dubai and thus microeconomic forces have reduced its market value somewhat.

The Dubai dream has moved away from mere financial reward and the city has heralded itself as a place to live the "ultimate" lifestyle. A long-exiled Springbok working in the hospitality industry explained Dubai's allure for both expats in general and his countrymen in particular: "Some South Africans think they have died and gone to heaven when they get to Dubai. Imagine a place where you get instant respect simply because you're white, regardless of your ability to do the job or your qualifications. They thought those days back home in South Africa were gone for ever. Also, there's an army of colored people here to put petrol in their cars, clean their houses, and cook their food: it's like the old days back home. They love it here!"

Although said partly in jest, this gives you a little insight into the attractions of expatriate life in Dubai. But a western expat can hire cheap housemaids anywhere in Asia and while never having to iron a shirt again has a certain appeal, this alone does not a utopia make. Property has been a key factor in transforming the way expatriates view their new lives far away from home. When Dubai passed a law in the 1990s that allowed foreigners to buy property, it changed the expat Monopoly board in the Gulf completely. Previously, expats shuffled around from place to place, chasing the money until they passed GO and collected what they needed to retire. Once expats were allowed to buy a home, they were invested in the result of the game.

In terms of the real estate industry in the UAE, Dubai's decision to let foreigners buy property was akin to Martin Luther nailing his list of demands to the door of Wittenberg Cathedral. Seemingly a modest act, Dubai was metaphorically putting up two fingers to the other emirates and the country's constitution, as selling land to non-nationals was illegal at the time. Dubai has always been somewhat self-centered, putting its own needs ahead of the rest of the UAE. By plowing its own furrow, it sought to please the foreigners it needed to drive its new-age economy, dependent on finance and hospitality rather than oil.

As a result, Dubai became the first place in the Gulf to really empower foreign workers by allowing them to own their own home, rather than treating them as disposable labor condemned to an eternity of renting. Over 100,000 people abandoned their overcast lives in Britain for a brightly hued home in Dubai. In the long term, the children of western expats may stay on to go to university or start their own careers, bypassing their homeland altogether to become second-generation expats. Just as importantly, property owners also received a residency visa independent of their local employers, who otherwise exercised almost feudal control over their staff. This simple act removed the "guest worker" status (no matter how pampered) that is the lot of most middle-class expatriates living in the Gulf. As a result, a generation of expats began to put down deeper roots than those who went before them. It was time to see at first hand the places Dubai's new generation of expats were calling home.

I started at the top. The Palm Jumeirah is home to some of the city's most expensive villas and apartments. This exclusive suburban address, far away from the back alleys of Deira and the Indian enclaves of Bur Dubai, feels like a different country; in many ways it is.

I had previously only seen the Palm Jumeirah from the skies. The background to its construction involved one of the many man-versus-nature battles that Dubai seems to thrive on. With only 70 kilometers of natural waterfront and little room to construct a high-end property market, Sheikh Mohammed issued the order to simply make some more. Despite sighs from environmentalists, the city gave the green light to create 500 kilometers of new waterfront property, with further plans to dump even more sand into the Gulf in the future. On its opening to residents, the developer (with customary modesty) declared the Palm Jumeirah to be "The Eighth Wonder of the World."

To take a peek inside the homes on the Palm, I needed to arrange a tour with a property agent. So, posing as a potential customer, I made a few phone calls to some of the many agents advertising in the local press. Pretty soon, a Range Rover was dispatched to pick me up, chauffeured by a convivial Nepalese named Anil. Although home for him had been a thatched hut without electricity in a village a couple of days' trek from Kathmandu, his job now involved ferrying the world's wealthy around to view the latest high-end property Dubai had for sale. Our journey took us out of the old city of Bur Dubai along Sheikh Zayed Road past the suburbs of Jumeirah.

Our first stop was to collect the estate agent. Before we picked her up, Anil gave me the inside scoop: "She came here only a few years ago from Kazakhstan with nothing.

But now she has a car and a flat, everything. The commissions are so big!" Flicking through the company's catalog, I could see what he was talking about. Even a tiny commission on some of the multimillion-dollar properties on offer would be a tidy sum. The last person to join us before we made our way out to the Palm Jumeirah was an Iranian representative from the developer.

After passing through security, we drove up the "trunk" of the "palm." All around us the building work was still far from finished, despite the fact that the u/c tag (under construction) had been removed from the official city map published by the municipality. We pulled up outside the first apartment building they had lined up for my delectation. A thick summer haze had descended and as soon as we alighted, my glasses fogged up. I was momentarily blinded. After wiping off the lenses, I was surprised to see some figures sprawled on the ground by my feet. Closer inspection revealed a number of men asleep on pieces of cardboard, while others were napping in some unfinished flower beds nearby. Again, Anil shone a light. These workmen were complying with a recent law prohibiting outdoor work between 12 a.m. and 3 p.m. during the summer months, when the heat is at its most intense. Since they were bussed in from labor camps such as Sonapur each morning, they simply flopped down wherever they could when their break time came. We stepped around a few of them, spread-eagled on the ground with their eyes closed, and went inside to inspect this little bit of heaven on earth.

The apartments themselves were modern, but for the amount of money involved, I had expected a bit more space. From the balcony you could see rows of villas on the outer "fronds," wedged unnervingly close together. As we walked through each room, the Iranian salesman described the amenities that were still forthcoming, including a desperately needed new shopping mall and a hotel on the outer verges of the Palm. There, or so went the rumors, is where a casino could be opened at some time in the future, the argument being that since the "frond" in question does not actually touch the coastline of Dubai, the casino in question could technically be labeled "offshore."

For all its claims to be the eighth wonder of the world, I could see why cynics had given the Palm a less grandiose title (or epitaph): "The World's Greatest Pile of Sand Ever Dumped in the Sea with Too Many Overpriced Houses Stuck on Top Cheek by Jowl." Outside, the private beach tried hard to impress, but there was no escaping the fact that it was simply a flat piece of sand beside an equally flat piece of water. When I thought about the windswept miles of glorious beaches and dunes my brothers and I had careered across as children in the west of Ireland, there was simply no comparison. These sentiments were best expressed by a Lebanese woman, who also found Dubai lacking in the sweeping natural grandeur that can take one's breath away. "Men built Dubai, but God made Lebanon!" she said, wistfully recalling the mountains and forests for which her homeland is famed. Though there was no shortage of sand or sun, something on the Palm Jumeirah just didn't feel right.

There is a similar sense of artificiality about much of Dubai's new suburban landscape. I didn't see much grass inside a development called The Meadows, for example. At the entranceways to the many other subdivisions I visited during my tour of New Dubai, Nepalese security guards measured out their lives in license plates, noting down the number as each car passed through. Inside, the city's expatriates get to live out their Dubai dreams in something that resembles Florida, just without the springy sod in the front lawns and the occasional hurricane.

Bringing gated communities to the Middle East is seen by some social theorists as a classic case of overkill, as the UAE is one of the safest countries in the world for middle-class professionals. Crime and violence against this stratum of society are rare. While cultural purists may bemoan the introduction of western anthropological practices to the region, putting a big wall around your property was a feature of life in Arabia long before the American sub-division was even invented. When the first pilgrims set out from Plymouth for the New World, houses in this part of the globe were already "gated" in some form or other. The traditional design of an Arabian home involved covered windows and a central courtyard where the women of the house could move about away from prying eyes, uncovered yet unseen. And up until the first half of the twentieth century, the city walls of Muscat, Kuwait, and Doha were locked each night – the ultimate in gated communities. Even the Nepalese security men manning the gates have anthropological antecedents. To this day, one of the most satisfying elements to communal living in the region is the presence of a *haris* or *bawab* (guard or gatekeeper) for every property.

Behind the walls western expats pass lives of relative ease and comfort, with a large underclass ready to perform the more menial tasks. There is sunshine for most of the year, perfect weather for that boat or convertible that would be impossible to run in England. But this gilded existence doesn't come without a price. Dubai's new generation of computer specialists, landscape engineers, and customer service managers have to sing for their supper. While career opportunities are good and management positions come around more quickly than back home, employers definitely extract a pound of flesh from the westerners they employ. Most expatriates aren't here "on a jolly," as a British acquaintance put it. In the good old days, a man of standing could come to Arabia and pick up a position that would have him clocked off by two and down the club by three. Today, after a long day's work Dubai's new generation of expats face a snail-paced commute in their sports cars back to their suburban homes. Given the inevitable demand, paradise was always going to suffer from congestion.

Yet there is more to Eden than endeavor. Once the work week is over, it's time to avail yourself of the entertainment that marks this city apart from its neighbors. On this particular Friday evening, the John Bull Pub was busy. With chicken tikka masala on the menu, fizzy European lager on tap, and a dartboard in the back, this little boozer had everything a homesick Englishman might need to feel at home.

Although it was still early doors, the two men sitting beside me at the bar had clearly been making themselves comfortable for some time. Their humor was rich and consisted of much good-natured ribbing at the expense of their respective homelands. India's recent cricketing defeat of England was the main source of merriment. Raj was in his late twenties, while Rob was fast approaching his half century. The two of them were partners in a growing business and they were here to let off a little steam. But they didn't want to talk about work: their main preoccupation was where to go next. And after an hour in their company, they were gracious enough to invite me along.

"What about the Continental?" Raj offered.

"No, we don't want to go there, that's a glorified whorehouse," Rob shot back. "If it's good music we want, it's got to be the Ocean Vista, they've got the best band in town. They're a Filipino outfit, really good."

I had some reservations. Experience caused me to envision a covers band running through the obligatory rendition of "Hotel California," followed quickly by a Céline Dion medley. Regardless, Raj and Rob were good company and I was keen to tag along. Once we had settled on our destination, the next decision was transport. Raj insisted he was fine to drive, though reassurance only came once we were outside on the street. The traffic around us was crawling along at barely five miles an hour and there seemed little chance of us attaining a speed at which damage could be done to ourselves or anyone else.

As we drove through the crowded streets, still thronged with traffic well past midnight, the two of them sang along at full volume to an Air Supply album pumping out from the stereo; the dodgy karaoke had already started and we hadn't even made it to our destination. When we finally parked and got out, Rob decided a little detour was in order. "You've got to see this place," he said with a nudge and a wink to Raj, marshaling us across the street to a nearby hotel and a Tex-Mex-themed bar on the ground floor. Our passage was interrupted at the door by a bouncer. He took one look at my feet (and Rob's as well) and pointed to a sign hanging on the wall beside the door: "No sandals or national dress." The dreaded sandal police had struck again!

Five years previously, my first attempt to sample Dubai's nightlife had been similarly derailed because one member of our party had been inappropriately shod. Although such signs are commonplace in Dubai, the detailed application of the rule is a minefield of etiquette a nineteenth-century governess would have difficulty explaining to her charges. Sandals and the *kandura* are most definitely not allowed in the city's top nightclubs, the ones that cater primarily to westerners. However, as many of the five-star hotels in Dubai also welcome well-heeled Gulf Arabs, sandals are accepted in their restaurants and the more expensive cigar bars. It's the gray area between the two that can catch you out. And as a devotee of the open toe, I had to be on my guard. In some of the swankier restaurants, locals are allowed to wear sandals with their national dress, while nonlocals must wear shoes – all very perplexing. And the confusion really kicks up a notch when you ask people why such rules are in place. This being Dubai, there were of course several theories.

Analysis needs context and there are some preconceptions I must dispense with before we begin. By sandals, we are not referring to plastic flip-flops or other items of beachwear. Sumptuously designed Italian leather sandals can be found on the feet of men dressed in exquisitely tailored *kanduras* in all the best hotels in Dubai. Full "local dress" is the equivalent of a suit and tie, or with a few amendments a tuxedo. Therefore, there is no bias against the level of formality of the sandal *per se*. It's the kind of establishment where the aforementioned item of footwear is deployed that is the decisive factor.

As the sandal ban primarily applies to nightclubs, one school of thought argues that the proscription is designed to keep out any *shebab* (be they locals or from other Gulf countries) who might have trouble grasping the western idea of a nightclub. Confusion might occur in the form of a gaggle of females on a hen night, none of whom is actually a prostitute. Whereas in other parts of Dubai the word "nightclub" is often synonymous with "brothel," some establishments are simply places where people of both sexes go to drink, dance, and hook up, without any money changing hands. But if you took a young Saudi guy more accustomed to Dubai's red-light establishments and dropped him in a regular nightclub, he might have some difficulty understanding the subtle cultural differences between the two, especially if there's drink taken. The sandal ban could therefore be designed to stop him at the door.

Another theory is that the ban on sandals and national dress in nightclubs aims to preserve the honor of the local population, by forcing them to do their drinking and carousing in western clothes. Thus, in any establishment where clients might be expected to really cut loose, the *kandura* and the sandals that go with it are generally not allowed. One expat posited the idea that mobile phone video footage of "mad Arabs" getting down at a jungle night appearing on the internet would somehow constitute bad press. Given Dubai's penchant for branding, the image-conscious proposition is a very credible option, though a little pointless. If you want to dance or drink in a *kandura*, all you have to do is cross the creek to Deira, where no such rules seem to apply.

As Raj, Rob, and I walked back out to the street, I wasn't that disheartened. Somewhere deep inside a voice was telling me that I had little business frequenting places where sandals weren't allowed.

When we finally reached the Ocean Vista, the bouncer at the door didn't have a problem with us, or our feet. A solidly built Nigerian called Brendan far away from home, it was fitting that he had been named after an Irish saint beloved of sailors and travelers. (Legend holds that St. Brendan the Navigator discovered the Americas nearly 1,000 years before Columbus – Dubai isn't the only nation willing to believe its own hype.) Inside, the venue was a pick-and-mix assortment of revelers: American sailors on liberty from aircraft carriers docked in Jebel Ali Port; a fashionable Indian couple (the boy's protective arm never left his girlfriend's shoulder); older British men in their fifties rollicking away in glam-rock heaven; Indian bachelors grooving on the dance floor eyeing up the girls while holding hands with each other; a couple of working girls from China and Ethiopia (who left the punters alone unless they indicated otherwise); tiny Filipina waitresses who managed to put a drink in every empty hand; and a full-bellied Egyptian man sitting at a corner table drinking whisky.

Into this mix charged Raj and Rob. They were still in high spirits as we pushed through the heaving crowd. Raj (who is only around five foot five) managed to spill beer over the biggest person in the place, an imposing pneumatic Michelin Man of an American, whose pectorals were so inflated they looked as if they were about to pop. The Michelin Man was clearly not impressed. He pointed to his Harley Davidson t-shirt (which indicated an affiliation somewhere in Texas) and growled something menacing in Raj's direction. Raj was prepared to launch into an impassioned rebuttal, but in his present condition I reckoned it would do more harm than good. So I quickly ushered him away, while offering his apologies.

Although Raj was born in Dubai to Indian parents, he had obviously picked up some English habits along the way. As we pushed onward through the crowd, he peppered the air with shouts of "Wanker!" directed either toward the Texan or a gray-haired Brit attempting to play air guitar on the dance floor in time with the Filipino covers band.

As the night progressed, I asked Raj if he had any plans to make the jump to Canada or Australia, a path that so many Indians who live in the Gulf choose as their next career move. He had other plans: "No way! Dubai is the best place in the world for me." Life was good and his business was doing well; Rob offered the technical know-how while Raj provided the capital and exploited his array of local contacts. At the same time Rob was shouting in my other ear, telling me how he missed his friends in England. He was nevertheless philosophical about life in Blighty. "Where would you get this for free back home any night of the week?" he asked, looking around him with a large smile across his face.

At that moment, the band belted out the opening chords of another crowd pleaser and the two of them took to the dance floor arm in arm, swaying back and forth. The song also brought a young American woman to the floor. Dressed in jeans and a tight-fitting t-shirt, her somewhat sensuous display clearly transfixed two close-shorn American men standing beside me. Even after I introduced myself, their eyes never left the young woman, who was now moving frenetically, her eyes closed, lost in the music. Although they said they "worked in the port," their haircuts and youth marked them out as military men. I presumed they had given me the standard response military personnel are ordered to give when strangers approach them ashore.

Although Dubai has earned a reputation as a drink-fueled refuge of sin, it is displays such as this that really give some Islamists sleepless nights. A young woman dancing on her own can scare the daylights out of the region's religious fundamentalists, much more than prostitutes and booze. Whoring and carousing are timeless and as old as Methuselah, while the fleshpots of Egypt continue to see a steady flow of visitors from the Gulf. But public displays of uninhibited and *unharnessed* female sensuality, outside of established boundaries, give religious conservatives the jitters. Dancers, singers, performers, actresses, even prostitutes are all professionals and, though deemed beyond the pale, they are at least understood. "Normal" women, the kind who make suitable wives, are not supposed to act in such an unrestrained manner, especially in public and in front of strange men. As long as it is only foreign women acting thus, though, the voices of religious conservatism should remain quiet.

Toward the end of the night, the band put on a virtuoso display of musicianship by swapping instruments and launching into a rousing closing rendition of Pink Floyd's "Shine On You Crazy Diamond," belting it out with both gusto and verve. And looking around at the eclectic confluence of nationalities momentarily forming a single amorphous mass, the choice of lyric seemed entirely apt for the location.

11

East of Eden

IT'S RAMADAN, THE HOLY MONTH OF FASTING FOR MUSLIMS, and I'm in the courtyard of a mosque in Bur Dubai with about a hundred other men. We're sitting cross-legged on dusty rugs on the ground, drinks and food laid out in front of us, waiting for the *adan*. Once the call to prayer rings out at sunset, we can eat; until then, we sit and wait. Observing the fast in the summer heat is certainly a test of devotion. During this month, the Islamic creed dictates that no water or food may be taken between sunrise and sunset. Along with the *shahada* (the profession of faith that there is no God but Allah and Mohammed is his messenger), *zakat* (giving alms), *salat* (praying five times a day), and *hajj* (making the pilgrimage to Mecca), fasting during Ramadan is one of the five pillars of Islam, religious obligations that all believers are meant to observe.

Amid all the revelry and carousing, it is easy to forget that at the core, this is an Islamic city. Once you peel away the layers of outside influence, it is Islam that remains. The call to prayer, evoking the name of Allah and his prophet Mohammed, rings out from both the minarets of the city's mosques and inside some of the glitzier shopping malls. That said, Dubai is a world away from the neighboring theocracies of Saudi Arabia and Iran. On the surface, many of the cultural restraints that bind personal behavior in other Gulf countries have been cut. But appearances should never be confused with reality. And for one month a year, Dubai remembers that sometimes where you came from is just as important as where you are going.

However, if you left Dubai with the perception that Ramadan is simply a month of self-deprivation and quiet introspection, you would be gravely mistaken. Once the sun goes down a festive mood prevails. While the holy month calls for Good Friday-like abstinence during daylight hours, the evenings resemble a succession of Christmas Eves. Lavish meals are served at sunset for *iftar*, the meal that breaks the fast each day. All the best television shows and films are shown during this month and there is a continual round of social engagements to attend. Children and young women get to stay out later than usual, while shops remain open till the early hours.

For many locals, life becomes inverted and day gets turned into night, getting up around 4.30 a.m. to eat a meal before sunrise and then returning to bed. As locals tend to work primarily in government ministries, bureaucracy can slow to a snail's pace. The work day over, a nap sees out the rest of the afternoon. A brisk stroll or a game of football occupies the last difficult hour before the *adan* rings out at sunset, signaling the end of the day's fast. This is when families gather and eat. Though the Prophet Mohammed advised dates and milk as the best way to break the fast, a five-course slap-up meal is *à la mode* nowadays. Closer to midnight, there is another meal called *sohur*, where the region's famed sweet tooth gets full expression in symphonies of seasonal sugary treats. In a touch of incongruity, many Muslims (and Christians and Hindus as well) gain weight during Ramadan – just imagine the effects on the waistline of eating a Christmas dinner every day for a month.

Non-Muslims are not obliged to fast, but the laws of the state are still deployed in order to protect the religious sensibilities of those who do. Restaurants and bars are closed during daylight hours and it is forbidden to smoke or drink in public. Bottles of water and cigarettes are rarely seen, except in the hands of tourists unaware of the expectations and constraints of the holy month. Rather than arrest people for violating the ban, the police generally warn any transgressors that it is illegal to eat and drink during daylight. If someone who is reminded of the law then refuses to desist, the authorities may not be so forgiving.

Pragmatism is the dominant ideology in Dubai and the city is always ready to compromise. Hotels still serve meals (though often behind curtains) to travelers and you can drink enough water to avoid dehydration in the aqua parks or on the golf course. From a theologian's perspective, Dubai is on fairly solid ground in allowing these concessions. The Koran makes provision for a number of exceptions to the fast: travelers, menstruating women, children, the elderly, and the infirm. In general, tourists and non-Muslims are not going to be arrested simply for eating or drinking, especially if there are no locals around to object. Just like its justice system, Dubai is content to live in a world of cultural schizophrenia. As long as any non-compliance is confined to areas where nonbelievers congregate, everything should be tickety-boo. On Jumeirah public beach, for example, where I saw foreigners working on their tans during the holy month, Ramadan was a custom honored both in the breach and the observance.

For the non-Muslims who make up such a large percentage of Dubai's population, Ramadan is either an inconvenience or simply a quaint anachronism. It is not something that should stop you taking advantage of a sunny weekend. As expatriates account for over 90 percent of private-sector employees, westerners often only glimpse the intricacies of Ramadan from a distance. The most difficult observance is the smoking ban, but office workers in need of a puff can usually find refuge in a basement store-

room or closet, where they can congregate for an illicit cigarette. They may even have some believers for company.
Overall, as long as you don't blow smoke in the face of a
passing policeman desperately counting the hours until he
can light up, everything should be all right.

Yet one shouldn't bank on unlimited understanding.
And what counts as acceptable behavior in the expat
enclaves of New Dubai might not always be welcome in
other parts of the city. Female tourists in shorts and sleeveless t-shirts slugging on their water bottles outside the
Grand Mosque will get strange looks, as such behavior con-
tradicts not one but two requests made of the faithful during the holy month. Along with refraining from food,
drink, and sex during *al-sawm* (the fast), the mind is supposed to remain free from thoughts of an erotic nature in
order to better contemplate the magnificence of God.
Exposed female flesh is thought to interfere with this
process for some reason. So women are asked to dress
modestly and refrain from wearing perfume or make-up, as
these accoutrements of female beauty provoke carnal
desires in the minds of men. The authorities are prepared
to accept a degree of give-and-take on such issues, even if
the prevailing winds in the Middle East are pushing for less
accommodating interpretations of Islam. The default setting for Dubai is tolerance, of both belief and ignorance.

Breaking the fast at *iftar* is generally a family affair done
communally at home. But for many low-income immigrant
bachelors, the fast is broken at various mosques around
the city – Islamic charities offer free meals each evening
throughout the month. Such generosity is partly inspired
by the belief that any charitable deeds performed during
Ramadan score significantly higher "points" with the
Almighty. As a result, there is generally an increase in charitable donations during this time. The mosque I was

visiting was one such place, where members of a local charity were seeking heavenly blessings by feeding the needy.

Suspicion (paranoia is probably a better word) is never far away when making journalistic enquiries in Middle East countries. Thus a modicum of discretion is advised when investigating anything that may be considered sensitive. Experience had taught me the best course of action: approach the person in the highest position of authority and affably (but humbly) seek their assistance. In the car park, large cauldrons of rice and meat were being unloaded from a van for the upcoming meal, while a number of local men in white *kanduras* roved around overseeing the proceedings. I didn't hold up much hope of slipping in among the crowd unnoticed (my preferred method of garnering information), while adopting my best I-was-just-on-my-way-to-the-mosque swagger wasn't going to work either.

After deciding which of the *kanduras* appeared the most senior, I walked up and introduced myself. I asked if he was the *mudeer* (manager). Replying in the affirmative, an ID inspection and a question-and-answer session ensued to establish my bona fides. Once the *mudeer* had reassured himself that I had some understanding of what was going on, he invited me to join the men for dinner. "But wait for the *adan*," he added, worried I might commit some ghastly solecism by falling on the food and stuffing my mouth before the due time. He also urged me "to write good about Islam," conscious of a possibly critical eye.

Once seated, a quick vox pop revealed that all the men around me were from India. But no one was in the mood to chat. They were all far more concerned with the five minutes that remained until it was time to eat. Despite the welcome, I knew I had overstepped the mark on this occasion and was now an unwelcome gatecrasher at someone else's party. When the *adan* finally rang out, it was a relief.

Rice and meat consumed, I made my way back out to the street, stopping to say goodbye to the *mudeer*. "Inshallah, you will become a Muslim," he said optimistically as we shook hands. But then something in my demeanor must have given him cause for reflection. He held my gaze for a few seconds. "How many years have you lived in the Middle East?" he asked. Although he didn't say anything else, the resigned look on his face seemed to say, "If we haven't got you by this stage, there's no hope for you now."

Sharjah, in many ways, is the Islamic conscience of both Dubai and the United Arab Emirates. Nudging up against the eastern side of Dubai's urban sprawl, it is known as the sober emirate. Alcohol is illegal, shops close on Fridays during the *dhur* midday prayers, and women are not allowed to wear sleeveless dresses. Along with the prohibition on alcohol, the porcine emporiums ("For Non-Muslims Only") that you find in Dubai's supermarkets are also absent. These restrictions, along with the emirate's "decency laws" (unmarried men and women may not congregate together), make Sharjah a lone beacon of Islamic temperance in the otherwise permissive UAE.

For anyone wishing to learn about Islamic culture and history in the UAE, this is also the place to go. Courtesy of its current ruler Sheikh Sultan Bin Mohammed Al Qasimi (a double PhD holder from Durham and Exeter), Sharjah has become the region's epicenter of Islamic history. Numerous museums and cultural institutions are within its borders, the centerpiece of which is the Islamic Museum or Madhaf Al Islami. For the conspiratorially inclined, Sharjah is a reminder of how Dubai could have turned out (or could be in the future) if a religiously conservative ruler had taken the helm of Maktoum Inc. Thus, when trying to imagine a Dubai that embraces faith-inspired prohibition, the simplest course of action is to abandon the city for a day and make a pilgrimage eastwards to Sharjah. (Both the spelling and pronunciation of Sharjah are howlers, by the way. The *j* should, according to the Arabic, be spelt with a ق *qaaf*, which is usually transliterated into English as a *q*. Sharqah literally means "easterly.")

Despite the fact that Sharjah is now practically a suburb of Dubai, I had postponed making the journey on a number of occasions. My hesitancy was greatly influenced by the congested bus stop near Baniyas Square. The queue stretched all the way down one street, around a corner, and on to the next. Here, the economic backwash of the Indian subcontinent stood dutifully each day in the heat, sweating their turn to join the congested drive home. Since parts of Sharjah are closer to downtown Dubai than suburbs such as Jebel Ali, it has become a home for many Dubai commuters, turning the main road between the two emirates into an infamous backlog of delays and traffic jams.

Dubai has countered the inevitable strain on its transport system by allowing the entrepreneurial spirit of the Indian subcontinent to step in and sort things out. While I was passing through Baniyas Square one day, a couple of men stood crying out the names of various destinations to the hordes milling about in the burning afternoon sun. One name stood out in particular: "Sharjah! Rolla Street, Sharjah! Rolla, Rolla, Rolla, Rolla!" Dubai's unofficial taxi market had stepped in and offered me an easier way eastward. I took a place with a group of other would-be commuters, standing in the shade of an office building, who bemoaned the lack of public transport. A minute later we were in the back of a Toyota Corolla heading to Sharjah.

A man with a briefcase placed across his lap introduced himself as Salman. Born in India, he had lived in Dubai in the mid-1990s before moving to the US. As he was now an American citizen, his employers in New York (who were looking to break into the Dubai market) believed that he was the natural choice to send as their representative. Salman, however, wasn't that impressed: "Nobody in these government departments knows who is responsible for this project. I've been back and forth between here and Abu Dhabi so many times. The people here in Dubai say it's a federal issue, but then the people in Abu Dhabi say it's a local issue." While Dubai prides itself on having moved beyond the bureaucratic hoop jumping that is part of everyday life in the rest of the Arab world, was this a little of the old way of doing things still hanging on? Or was the UAE's federal system of governance throwing a bureau-cratic spanner in Dubai's well-greased works? Salman also didn't like the changes over the last decade and couldn't imagine moving back here. "Do you know what the price of one room can be, even out in Sharjah? They want crazy money for just one room where you share a bathroom with eight other guys. There's a schedule for a shower in the morning, if you miss your time slot, that's it, no shower for you! Live in Dubai now? No chance!"

That said, the US didn't feature in his future plans either: "In the States, you have to work way too hard, there is no free time. People don't have a life! Private education is very expensive and the public school system is garbage." Airport security had become a particular annoyance: "Flying internally in the States is a nightmare now. The security guards take one look at me and say something into their radios. Then it takes ages for me to get anywhere. I'm fed up with the place." Salman insisted that anyone with a Muslim name was looked on with suspicion and he was sick of being regarded as a potential terrorist every time he flew. His future lay to the east: "I'm going back to India. There I can give my son a good education and after that he can do as he likes."

By now we had left Dubai behind and were passing through the Al Nada Interchange, an eerie oasis of cold concrete where the two emirates merge seamlessly into one another. As property prices rose, many people began to see Sharjah as a place to live cheaply while enjoying the bene-fits of a Dubai wage. This demographic shift led to its own property boom. As we drove into Sharjah, we saw numer-ous high-rise buildings in various states of completion sil-houetted against the sky. Amid all these new buildings, the one incongruous item was a tall Ferris wheel, a London Eye to pass away an Arabian weekend.

Salman was unimpressed. In the US, he had worked in quality control for a large construction firm and his profes-sional view of the building work wasn't very high: "There is a problem with the soil here, and the foundations. The soil-bearing foundation is not right. The life of the smaller build-ings, up to seven stories, is about 23–27 years maximum, from seven stories up maybe 32 years. Then, they're going to need some very expensive work on the foundations. It will probably be cheaper just to knock them down."

It was from an RAF aerodrome in Sharjah that Thesiger flew back to Britain and "exile," when he hung up his camel saddle and called time on his Arabian travels. In his view, Sharjah wasn't up to much:

[It was] as drab and as tumble-down as Abu Dhabi, but infinitely more squalid, for it was littered with... piles of

empty tins, broken bottles, coils of rusting wire, and fluttering bits of paper... discarded rubbish which had been mass produced elsewhere.

Nearly 60 years later, though some of the details may have changed, much of the city left me with a similar impression. In the interim, as Dubai and Abu Dhabi prospered, Sharjah remained the poor relation, even after discovering natural gas in the 1980s. Though there were some islands of elegant construction, there was a worn and weary feel to much of the city. The fort in the center looked lonely. Marooned inside a roundabout, it was a temporal refugee in an ocean of sickly concrete. Even the city's many historical buildings had been renovated so thoroughly that they were almost unrecognizable to those who knew them in their original state. Unlike Dubai, which spends its money on bling, Sharjah had taken a more sober route. It is more famous for schools and universities than shopping malls or skyscrapers.

When compared to Dubai and Abu Dhabi, there is no doubt that Sharjah has lagged behind its Bani Yas friends of late, no doubt influenced by the turbulent transitions of power it has witnessed in its recent history. Unlike the smooth continuity seen in Dubai – only four rulers in the last 100 years – Sharjah has been Coup City since the Second World War. A certain Saqer Bin Sultan became the ruler in 1951, only to be deposed (supposedly with British involvement) in 1965 by Khalid III Bin Muhammad. Saqer then fled to Cairo, returning in early 1972 with his own counter-coup. During this attempted takeover, the palace was stormed and Khalid III was killed. Unfortunately for Saqer, he wasn't allowed to hang about for very long before the British sent him into exile again. If all this reads like the stuff of an adventure novel, such shenanigans were indeed recounted in classics such as *The Black Camels of Qashran*, which tells a very similar tale (although the novel was actually published two years before the real events occurred). The last coup took place in 1987, when a brother of the incumbent seized power for six days. After the ruling family held an emergency meeting, they decided to restore power to Sheikh Sultan, with the understanding that some changes would be made in the way the public purse was divvied up.

This kind of turmoil cannot be good for business. Looking around at the long line of little shops selling an assortment of bric-à-brac on Rolla Street, I wondered if Dubai's progress grated the locals here in Sharjah at all, as they ride their Ferris wheel and look along the Gulf toward their flashier neighbor. In the last half-century Dubai has become a regional business hub, despite Sharjah stealing a lead on all the local competition.

In the 1930s, Sharjah secured landing rights for Britain's Imperial Airways to land its seaplanes here. This was seen as an unusual move at the time, as the ruling family were cousins of the Al Qasimi clan in Ras Al Khaimah, who had a history of hostility toward the British Empire. Ultimately, the relationship between them didn't last and the British moved their base to Dubai, rather than expanding their imperial presence in Sharjah, creating an interesting urban legend in the process. The story goes that on hearing that the British were keen to increase their operations in Sharjah, the Sheikh of Dubai warned his more conservative counterpart in Sharjah that such an expansion would bring about an influx of western (and thus un-Islamic) practices: women would be going around uncovered and there'd be gin everywhere! Supposedly, once the Sheikh of Sharjah declined the British request, the ruler of Dubai quickly stepped in and offered his home town as an alternative air strip.

Evidence of Sharjah's residual religious conservatism was visible as soon as I took to the streets. A sign outside one mosque announced: "Entrance to the mosque is restricted for Muslims only." This is generally an unspoken rule in much of the Gulf; it was telling that Sharjah spelt out the prohibition so directly. Although I had only journeyed a matter of miles from Dubai, I sensed temporal (as well as spatial) disparities. The Arabian *yin* and *yang* that greets visitors on arrival at Dubai International Airport (men in white working alongside women in black) was missing one half of the equation. The streets of Sharjah were devoid of white *kanduras*; local women were the main force. Dressed in black *abayas* (loose black robes worn over clothes to hide the female form), they moved slowly along the pavements in groups of three or four.

Although all were covered, they represented the gamut of what constitutes conservative dress in the Gulf. One wore a black *niqab* that concealed her face, leaving only her eyes exposed *à la* Dick Turpin. Another sported a veil draped over her entire head, creating somewhat of a beekeeper effect. Behind them came a teenager, with a *sheala* (a loose headscarf worn to conceal the hair) draped casually on her head and exposing some hair at the front – a demi-*hejab* of sorts. An elderly lady took one look at me and ordered the young woman in her charge to rearrange her *sheala* to cover all of her hair. Women born into these societies will tell you that by only partially covering her hair the youngest of this group was acting in deference to traditional Bedouin sensitivities, rather than Islamic ones. A *muhajba*, a woman who covers her hair for religious reasons, would not expose so much as a strand.

When it comes to the social mores of the Middle East, no issue gets westerners as worked up as the covering/non-covering of women, despite our own tendencies toward anthropological schizophrenia in this matter. When the first Christian missionaries landed in Africa, they were shocked by the nudity they encountered and implored the natives to put some clothes on. Nowadays, when enlightened libertarians from the West come to the Muslim world, they insist that women need to throw off their veils. What is a girl to do?

For a western woman newly arrived in Dubai, the issue of when or how to cover one's body and hair can be a little confusing, but be reassured there are a number of choices open to you. One approach is to wear the skimpiest shorts available, accompanied by a tiny see-through top, and carry on regardless. As long as you don't mind being stared at, you should be all right. The other involves modifying your appearance to avoid exposing too much flesh. However, you are strongly advised *not* to do the following: wear groin-clinching shorts topped with a bikini exposing a vast amount of cleavage and then decide to put a veil over your hair in an attempt to be culturally sensitive. That would be like a reformed heroin addict showing up at his twelve-step program taking hits off a crack pipe and declaring: "Hey, look at me! I've been clean for five months!"

A Saudi acquaintance once told me that Allah has reserved a special place in paradise for the inventor of the air-conditioner. At this moment, I would have recommended beatification. Inside the Madhaf al Islami, the ice-cold air was a glorious relief after the blistering heat I had endured outdoors. The collection of artifacts included a gold-embroidered covering of the Kabba in Mecca and a stone that bore the seal of the Prophet – *Mohammed Rasoul Allah*. Although everything carried a tangible sense of history, overall the experience left me a little cold. There was far too much repetition and not enough interaction for my liking. As an introduction to Islam, this was in complete contrast to a previous visit I had made to Dubai's main Islamic tourist attraction, the Jumeirah Mosque. Not only had it scored some extra points for simply letting me inside, the tour was interactive and fun, while the Madhaf Al Islami was all one-way traffic.

In Jumeirah, a pair of chirpy British *muhajba* women (presumably married to local men) wearing *abayas* and *shealas* (no hair exposed) had delivered a straightforward Islam 101 seminar to an assembly of international tourists, some of whom were only on a brief stop-over while in transit to elsewhere. The women covered all the basics, thoroughly charmed the audience, and answered a range of questions without reserve, though with occasional inaccuracy. As one of them held up a large photograph of Mecca, the other explained that this city in Saudi Arabia was the place of pilgrimage for Muslims. When a man in the crowd asked if there were any other places of pilgrimage in Islam, one of the women replied in the negative. If you asked a Shiite Muslim that question, you would get a very different answer, as visiting the holy cities of Karbala and Najaf in Iraq is a major part of the Shia faith. For a moment, the know-it-all gene inside me sprung to attention and I was tempted to pitch in, but I stayed quiet. The women were doing an excellent job combating the lack of understanding in much of the world today. However, I did bite my tongue when one of them told us that the word Islam means "peace." Although linguistically accurate, "submission" (to God's will) is the accepted theological translation.

When I had finished with the museum, there seemed little reason to remain in Sharjah. Not having any plans to return any time soon, I wanted to pick up a souvenir before saying goodbye. Culture, though often cherished through a nation's history, is nowadays more commonly expressed through shopping. For the Sharjah visitor there is ample culture on sale at the Souk Al Arsa, but the stifling heat was doing a good job of keeping the tourists away. Even the shop owners had abandoned the place, leaving their teenage sons in charge during the slow summer months.

One shop in particular caught my eye. The walls were decked with a wide selection of *jambeeyas*, curved ornamental daggers from Yemen. It was here I met young Ibrahim. An Emirati citizen, his father had originally come from Yemen. Ibrahim was assisted by the equally charming Imran, a Muslim from northern India. We talked for over an hour. Having spent much of the previous week inside my own head, their easy company was gladly welcomed. As I readied to leave, I finally settled on a set of *nisbah* (prayer beads) as my *memento mori* of Sharjah. Imran explained that the beads weren't to be used simply as a plaything to keep your hands busy, and recounted the specific prayer that should accompany their use. Just then, the *adan* sounded for the evening prayer.

Over the next few minutes, people began to make their way out toward the mosque located just outside the *souk* for the last prayer of the day. Ibrahim asked if I would care to join him. As we walked out into the sweltering night air, I declined his offer. In the Gulf not every invitation is meant to be accepted. I thanked him, but reminded him of the sign warning that only Muslims were allowed inside mosques. He was quick to dismiss this prohibition as nonsense. Although he identified me as a *messihi* (Christian), this did not bother him in the slightest. "Since we pray to the same God, why can't we pray in the same place?" he asked.

Again I declined and bade him farewell. As he walked toward the open door of the mosque, where people were already gathering inside, I took a seat on a nearby bench. I knew that my presence inside would make people uncomfortable. As I watched the slow trickle of people make their way inside the mosque, the extreme distance that exists between non-Muslims and the local culture in much of Arabia was brought home to me. No matter how close you get to people who live here, if you don't share one of the core bonds of either family or religion, you'll always be on the outside looking in, your nose pressed against the glass. Without blood ties, friendships with locals in the Gulf can be somewhat anemic, as ultimately it's family that counts. As such, many of the friendships foreigners forge with people here tend to be with young people. Adults with their own families often have precious little time for anyone else. Even Bin Kabina and Bin Ghabaisha, to whom *Arabian Sands* is dedicated, were paid to accompany Thesiger on his travels and were only teenagers at the time.

A little downhearted, I came away from the *souk* and went down to the nearby docks. A long line of ships had docked for the night, and bare-chested sailors were getting comfortable on the open decks. Rising up into the now darkened sky, an ornate mosque was illuminated in the muggy night air. But even here beside the water, there was little relief from the overpowering heat. The humidity was unrelenting and had turned Sharjah into a vast outdoor steam room. After a few minutes, an initial sweat turned into a torrent. By the time I had reached the mosque I was a mess. My clothes were stuck to my skin, as if someone had doused me with a bucket of water, as greasy as the last piece of fried aubergine stuffed into a sandwich in an Arabic takeaway late in the afternoon. On reaching the mosque, I took out my camera. Immediately, the lens fogged up. All I could see was a hazy image shining dimly through the humidity. Cursing the weather and finally Sharjah itself, I turned on my heels and resolved to get back to Dubai as quickly as possible.

While I was waiting for a taxi, a brightly lit shack across the street caught my attention. Crossing over to peep inside, I saw three men sitting around a large curved hotplate, engaged in some culinary activity I had never seen before. After one kneaded a fresh piece of dough into a circle, another slapped it onto the hot metal plate. Once the bread took shape, a triangle of processed cheese was placed on top before a raw egg was cracked onto the rapidly cooking bread. After a solid dousing with a dark brown fish sauce, the outsized but paper-thin sandwich was folded into a large semicircle and deposited on a plastic tray.

Although Afghans have built up a reputation for being fierce *mujahedeen* and Formula 1-inspired taxi drivers, my years in the Middle East had left me with other stereotypes. In Kuwait, Afghan bakers and cooks can be found in cooperative supermarkets across the country making delectable fresh flatbread and *ash* (a type of lentil stew). I asked the three men if this was an Afghan dish. "*La! La! La! Hadha Irani, moo Afghani!*" (No! No! No! This is Iranian, not Afghan!) was the chorused response, no doubt from a collective of culinary-aggrieved Iranians.

I ordered a sandwich and watched the cook repeat his magic. Then I took my tray and sat outside. The place certainly was popular and a good number of locals were coming in for a late evening snack. As I ate, a local man walked past. "Good, yes?" he enquired, smiling broadly. "*Mumtaz!*" (Excellent!) I replied and decided to order another, remembering at that moment, in spite of the differences of culture, religion, and Allah knows what else you may encounter in this part of the world, exactly what it is that keeps you coming back for more.

12

Dirty Linen

"ALL THIS BUILDING, IT IS FULL OF DIRTY MONEY," Yousef said, dismissing the mass of construction and roadworks around us with a wave of his hand. On either side, the road was littered with men and heavy machinery. Looking back toward the city, a line of skyscrapers in varying degrees of completion stretched to the clouds. My new-found companion wasn't impressed, however: "Russians, Colombians, from all over the world they come and buy property for cash. Then after a couple of months, they sell it on again, even for a discount! But then they get issued with a check, clean money they can then take anywhere in the world."

We had met barely ten minutes before in the lobby of my hotel. An elderly man, he was reclined comfortably in an armchair smoking a cigarette, gowned in the traditional Emirati *kandura* and *gutra* headdress. All it took was a "*Sabah al kher*" (good morning) on my part and we were off. When the conversation got around to my plans (I had an errand to run on the outskirts of town), Yousef sprang to his feet and insisted that he drive me there. He wouldn't dream of letting me take a taxi!

It is at times such as this that the traveler has a choice. Do you take a leap of faith, jump right in, and see where the road takes you? Or do you politely decline and keep your personal space intact? This was but one of many instances when Dervla Murphy's advice has proven most sapient: "In Asia, it is always a good idea to broadcast one's plans."

A few minutes later, we were driving away from the urban center and along the ring roads that circle the outskirts of the city. Once we had properly introduced ourselves, Yousef began to talk about his family. His first love had been history and literature – Milan Kundera and the Saudi novelist Turki Al Hamad were his favorites – and he insisted that the greatest gift he could give his children was a love of reading. Possibly due to our conversation, he briefly lost his way at an intersection, and cursed all the construction and development that had momentarily made him a stranger in his own country.

Once my business was complete (Yousef insisted on waiting), he drove me back to the hotel. There we spent a pleasant hour over coffee. An avid fan of local history, Yousef was equally bemused by Dubai's transformation from a sleepy sea town to the bustling metropolis it is today. His random act of kindness told me that all the recent development couldn't quench his culture's famed hospitality. However, both Interpol and the Federal Bureau of Investigation believe that Dubai could show a lot less hospitality to some of the global economy's shadier characters. The game today for many international criminals is to keep their money moving around the world faster than a police force can trace it. Dubai is just one stop on this financial whirligig and the city's property industry has been accused of embracing large quantities of illicit money. In much of the western world, buying a property outright in cash generally sets off a number of alarm bells and involves compulsory reporting of the purchase to the authorities. No such regulations exist in Dubai.

The city's reputation as a haven for unlawful goings-on is nothing new. Gun running and the slave trade (even after the British outlawed the practice) both found a welcoming home in the Gulf during the first half of the twentieth century. And in the 1950s and 1960s, Dubai became an important staging post for "re-exporting" gold across the Arabian Sea to India, where gold was heavily taxed.

Not surprisingly, India had a different name for this trade (smuggling), which must have been blessed by the highest echelons of Dubai society. Old sailing *dhows* were fitted out with powerful engines to outrun any overly curious patrol boats from the Indian navy. Displaying a keen business sense, those involved in the re-export trade thought it a shame for these ships to return to Dubai empty handed. But what kinds of goods were worth bringing back from places such as Iran, Pakistan, or India? Thus it came to pass that Dubai also became known as a transit point for opium and hashish on its way from Asia to Europe.

This is one part of Dubai's past that does not generally appear in official histories. But there is still a way to get a feel for the gold-smuggling trade, through a potboiler of a novel published in 1976, simply called *Dubai*. Written by Robin Moore (better known for *The French Connection*), the book is a classic piece of "sheikhploitation" and is worth buying for the blurb on the front cover alone:

> *Dubai: The hot spot... where adventurers play the world's most dangerous games... gold, sex, oil and war... A wild seething place in the sunbaked sands of Arabia, where billion-dollar carpet-baggers mix explosive passions with oil. And exotic pleasures pay fabulous dividends... where life is cheap and no price too high for pleasure.*

The character sketches on the back cover continue in a similar vein, from a dogged adventurer to a luscious dusky maiden and a lecherous sheikh of epic proportions:

> *FITZ: He contracted for a violent smuggling operation and made the hottest deal of his life...*
> *LAYLAH: The exotic beauty wanted more than any man could offer, but sold herself for less...*

SAQR: *The jaded prince whose sexual lusts were law in his ruthless empire...*

Though this was fiction, the usual disclaimer that the characters were the work of the writer's feral imagination wasn't swallowed by the Maktoum family, some of whom thought there was indeed quite a "resemblance to actual persons living or dead." This is one book that does not grace the shelves of the city's bookshops, though second-hand copies do float around among expats. Rumor has it that the publishing rights were bought up by a member of the Maktoum family, who then quietly allowed it to go out of print.

And even today, Dubai continues to attract people operating in the shadows. One such man was a former Soviet officer turned arms dealer named Victor Bout, better known as the Merchant of Death. While flying out of Sharjah and banking in Dubai, his clientele is alleged to have included Charles Taylor in Liberia (who would later face war crimes charges in The Hague); the Taliban in Afghanistan; and, more intriguingly, the US government and a host of relief agencies operating across Africa. Although he always claimed to be a legitimate businessman, the US government finally arrested Bout during a sting operation in Bangkok while he was (allegedly) selling surface-to-air missiles to undercover DEA agents posing as Colombian rebels.

Another of Dubai's more infamous residents was Dawood Ibrahim, king of the Mumbai underworld. Rising from a modest upbringing as the son of a policeman, Dawood led the D-Company crime syndicate, which over the years has been linked to drugs, smuggling, money laundering, and mass murder. After relocating to Dubai in the late 1980s, he turned to film production. Funding

Bollywood movies allowed him to fly in a steady stream of film stars and singers, and reports of lavish parties and a relationship with an actress made him the darling of the scandal sheets back home. But when India and the US started to complain about Dawood's activities (his organization was linked to a series of bombings in Mumbai in 1993), his days in Dubai were numbered. Dawood slipped out of the country to Pakistan. Since then, he has been accused of having links with groups such as Al-Qaeda, leading the US government to label him a "global terrorist." Furthermore, in the wake of a coordinated series of attacks on Mumbai in 2008 by Kashmiri separatists, the Indian government claimed that he was involved and demanded his extradition to Delhi. The lesson seems to be that if you are a shady character wanting to reside in Dubai, it is best not to wash your dirty linen in public.

There are other sins on offer. In Dubai you can shake off the various political, theological, and sectarian obstacles that can get in the way of having a good time in much of the Middle East. It only takes a quick glance at a regional map to see the attraction for would-be party goers. To the east is the revolutionary Islamic Republic of Iran, while to the west you find the Salafist Kingdom of Saudi Arabia. Other cities that dot the map – Basra, Baghdad, Busheir – are not cities that immediately spring to mind when planning a big night out. But in Dubai, a modern-day playground has sprouted from the sands.

This was a role previously filled by the Lebanese capital Beirut, whose former allure was summarized by the American journalist Thomas Friedman thus:

Beirut's banking secrecy, casinos, and wild, salacious nightlife... made it an attractive oasis for an Arab world... Every region of the globe needs one city where the rules don't apply, where sin is the norm, and where money can buy anything or anyone. Asia had Hong Kong, Europe had Monaco and the Middle East had Beirut.

Fifteen years of civil war, followed by another fifteen as a Petri dish for larger regional conflicts, saw Beirut cede the title to Dubai by a technical knockout. As a regional financial center Dubai has comfortably surpassed its Levantine cousin, but when it comes to hedonism it is still no Beirut. For the time being, gamblers have to settle for the *halal* casino of the stock exchange if they want a flutter. Recreational drugs are of course available, but Dubai has yet to spawn the sprawling cannabis plantations found in the Bekka Valley, producing diversionary tools such as Lebanese Blonde. Claims to decadence will always be muted until you have an illicit substance named in your honor. And while religious holidays are observed in multi-confessional Lebanon, bars in the Christian parts of the city aren't compelled to close in honor of Islamic holidays, as is the case in Dubai.

I came face to face with this particular prohibition one night when meeting Lincoln for a drink. His Dubai dream was throwing up more obstacles than he had expected and he seemed in need of a night out. However, our plans were stymied by a sign on the door of the bar we had in mind:

Pub will remain closed because of
Mawlid Al Nabi
From Friday 6.30 pm till Saturday 7.30 pm
Thank you

The occasion in question was the Prophet's Birthday, one of only two nights in the year (the other being Lailat Al Miraj or the Night of the Prophet's Ascension) when Dubai compels all bars to close. Some see this as merely paying lip service to religion, but it is a concept I am more than used to. In Ireland, public houses are also compelled to close two days a year (Christmas Day and Good Friday respectively) in a similar act of faith-inspired prohibition. Another American friend, who can be a fierce (but well-informed) critic of Arab society, once enumerated a long list of the faults he found in the region: religious hypocrisy, a tendency to resolve political injustice through violence, and religious figures who attempt to control the public by threatening damnation and hell fire, coupled with suffocating family structures than can give people little or no personal space. I must admit, it all sounded remarkably familiar!

But nature abhors a vacuum. Lincoln insisted that during his time in Bahrain, similar alcohol restrictions had been in place but were easily circumvented, if only you knew who to ask. "These guys should know something," he said, falling into conversation with a young Ethiopian who worked for the hotel in question. The man's name was Berihun and he told us he knew of a place. Luckily, he was clocking off soon and he offered to take us there. "We're not looking for girls," Lincoln added with a smile, "just a beer," mindful that in many parts of Africa (and much of Dubai, for that matter) the two go hand in hand.

A short taxi ride and a few phone calls later, the three of us were deposited in a Deira back street, in front of a ragtag collection of tumbledown apartment buildings. Lines of washing hung from the narrow balconies and a nearby skip was overflowing with rubbish. Berihun made another phone call. After a few minutes, a woman appeared in an agitated state pointing to one of the nearby buildings, but waving her hands and warning us off: "No! No! Not here! There's trouble up there now! Bad men!" My first instinct was to turn around and get out of there, but Lincoln was a reassuring presence. Berihun and the woman had a quick chat in Amharic. There was another option.

The woman guided the three of us toward another ramshackle building farther down the street. Once inside, we all crammed into a tiny lift. She tapped on a door on the fourth floor, which opened to a tiny apartment where five African men and a couple of women sat around a coffee table with a few cans of Heineken and a bottle of whisky. The "establishment" was run by two Ethiopian sisters. We found a spare seat in a corner and ordered a beer.

Berihun enlightened us regarding the sisters' customer base, generally other Africans unwilling to pay the high prices charged in Dubai's licensed premises. In Ireland there is a saying that there is no such thing as a poor publican and in Dubai this is equally so. Given the emirate's strategic location between two prohibitive (yet not necessarily abstemious) nations, a license to sell alcohol is a license to print money. Despite the city's reputation as a start-up-friendly bastion of economic liberalism, alcohol licenses are restricted to hotels, all of which must have a local partner. Freelancers like these two sisters circumvented the system by sourcing their alcohol from the neighboring emirate of Ajman, whose GNP seems to be derived exclusively from two hole-in-the-wall off-licenses selling discounted booze.

As we talked, two other Ethiopian women walked in and looked around; presumably they wanted to know if Lincoln's assertion that it was only beer we were after was still correct. They moved on once they established there was no custom coming their way.

If it is female company you want, you don't have to trawl through the speakeasies of Deira far from prying eyes. In Bur Dubai you can easily find a host of tacky disco bars where flesh is the main commodity on offer, even if the powers that be do a good job of covering it up. From the lobby, your hotel may seem the height of respectability. It's only from the street that you may see a second entrance, to a nightclub and manned by bouncers. Inside, beneath gleaming disco balls, such establishments offer a wall-to-wall rainbow coalition of young women from China, East Africa, and a host of former Soviet Republics, all actively vying for business. It's the sheer number that overwhelms you at first, a complete inversion of the standard Dubai demographic. The official ratio of men to women in Dubai is about 3:1, yet inside these clubs it's almost 1:2. Although economists might label this a case of drastic oversupply, the market price of labor is ultimately determined by nationality, just like in every other profession in the city. In these clubs, there is a sliding geographical scale running from 500 to 1,000 dirhams, starting with China, moving on to Africa, and then to the former Soviet states. Arabic-speaking *binat al hawa* (girls of the wind) from countries such as Morocco generally command the highest prices.

Supply-side economics was never my thing; the demand for goods and services is a much easier concept to grasp. The ongoing American military presence across the greater Middle East was certainly boosting this particular sector of the local economy. Despite the popular use of the term, it was difficult to label the absurdly young-looking American man I met on one occasion as a "mercenary." This 24-year-old veteran had exited the revolving door of the US military as a poorly paid grunt, only to walk straight back in earning six figures in the employ of a security contractor.

His new career entailed escorting convoys of diplomats around the Iraqi capital. Surprisingly, this was proving less stressful than his previous job: "I used to be in the Marines before. We fought in Fallujah, so Baghdad ain't that bad. And at least now the pay is a lot better." Dubai had become an important operations hub and transit point for military personnel and private contractors operating from Iraq to Afghanistan, and for all the ancillary services that spring up wherever military men go on leave.

After the Ethiopian sisters passed around a plate of beef stew and *injera* flatbread, Lincoln and I sat about catching up for an hour. Striking it rich was proving more difficult than he had expected. While there was no doubting his tenacity, Lincoln was on his own and thus the odds were stacked against him. Despite Dubai's wanton embrace of globalization, the forces that underpin many of its more successful enterprises are much less modern. Lincoln's friend Ahmad had his kinsfolk back in Iran to grease the wheels of commerce whenever they came unstuck; the Pathan taxi drivers lived eight to a room with their extended family and thus overcame an otherwise crippling rental market; and even these two sisters running their backstreet *shebeen* were using the timeless bonds only blood can bring to realize their dreams.

13
Secret Dubai Diary

Notification

It is hereby notified for public information that from the date hereof every person whoever he may be and whatever may be his position is forbidden from relating or conveying from me to the majlis or from the majlis to me any false words, talk or news, or in any way spreading agitating rumours. Any person who may disregard this notification shall be severely punished.

Dated 27th Sha'ban 1357, corresponding to 29th Oct., 1938.
Said bin Maktoum
Ruler of Dubai

IN THE HEART OF THIS ARABIAN METROPOLIS, inside a bright, airy building housing the Dubai Municipal Court, is where you find justice at work. Walking into an empty courtroom, I take a pew and wait for the day's proceedings to begin. The first person to join me is a young Emirati lawyer wearing a black *abaya* (which looks suspiciously like a barrister's robe). She pops her head in the door and asks me to move over to the other side of the room. I have inadvertently sat in the makeshift women's section. When the lawyer returns, she is followed by a tiny, fragile-looking Asian woman dressed in the blue uniform of a domestic servant.

Over the next few minutes, Courtroom Number 9 of the Dubai Municipal Court begins to fill up and it's time to get down to business. At nine o'clock precisely and to a distinctly authoritarian interjection, the judge enters. He is resplendent in a black robe and black *egal* worn over a gleaming white *gutra*. We all rise in honor of his honor.

Outside, a huge banner proclaimed that e-justice had arrived in Dubai, bringing levels of customer service to the legal system that wouldn't be out of place on an Emirates Airways flight. The corridors of the courthouse were patrolled by men wearing the green uniforms of the Ministry of Interior, the lion's share of whom come from the less economically robust neighboring countries, such as Yemen, Pakistan, and Oman. Outsourcing has compensated for the lack of interest among the local youth for plodding the beat.

Rubbing shoulders with the less savory aspects of the Dubai dream had disturbed my equilibrium somewhat. I had resisted an active pursuit of the dark side, since I wanted to give the place a fair shot at creating a good impression. After it all, it would be a little unfair if an Arab student of Irish culture arrived in Dublin exclaiming, "Okay, so let's start with that funny dancing you guys do and then we'll move on to those pedophile priests." But I hadn't gone looking for the other side of the Dubai dream, it had come to me; and the homeless Asian men sleeping on the pavements in Deira and the working girls of Bur Dubai were not to be simply airbrushed away.

I had heard rumors that the legal system in Dubai was a little drawn out, but on this occasion the judge could not be accused of torpidity. He rattled through the first five cases in half an hour. Most of the accused appeared to be locals. One side effect of Dubai's ruling bargain and cradle-to-grave welfare state has been a certain amount of disaffection and indolence among some sections of the emirate's youth. With little incentive to strive for success, idle hands are sometimes distracted by what the state sees as the devil's work. The accused were already in police custody, dressed in a remand uniform of white trousers and t-shirts. They had a somewhat browbeaten look as they were ushered into the courtroom through a door to the right of the judge. I didn't understand the curt Arabic, but in all five cases the word hashish got a mention. The young men didn't get much time in front of his Lordship before they were dispatched from whence they came. If they were going to face the full wrath of the penal code, I pitied them with a passion. The minimum sentence for possession of even a scintilla of cannabis is a mind-altering four years.

Dubai is proud of its "zero-tolerance" policy toward illegal substances. The frontline of this war on drugs is the airport and this has been the scene of many an arrest in recent years, some which have been positively Kafkaesque. The resulting headlines in the local and international press are a reminder that the Arabic expression *ya ghareeb kun adeeb* is just as important in Dubai as anywhere else in the region – a foreigner should be well behaved.

BRITON JAILED FOR FOUR YEARS IN DUBAI AFTER CUSTOMS FIND CANNABIS WEIGHING LESS THAN A GRAIN OF SUGAR UNDER HIS SHOE

JAIL TERM UPHELD FOR MAN WHO CARRIED TINY QAT LEAF

NZ GUITARIST JAILED FOR 0.7 GRAMS OF MARIJUANA

RADIO DJ JAILED IN DUBAI OVER DRUGS

MAN HELD FOR OVER-THE-COUNTER SLEEP MEDICINE

TRAVELERS WHO SMUGGLE "POPPY SEEDS" FACE JAIL IN DUBAI

Some of the above cases were resolved after a few months in custody. The victims were lucky enough to have friends who vociferously campaigned for their release. Others have not been so lucky. Hundreds languish in the UAE's notorious Al Watba prison, primarily because they do not have the means to launch an effective media campaign. Those who threaten to hit Dubai in the only place that really hurts (its pocket) tend to get the best results: "My Dubai Hell" is not the kind of headlines the tourism czars like to read in the British press.

Despite having a reputation for innovation in terms of architecture and design, when it comes to the criminal justice system some of Dubai's moral sensibilities can seem positively Victorian. Its capriciousness does not extend only to illegal substances; sexuality is policed in an idiosyncratic fashion:

17 "CROSS-DRESSING TOURISTS" HELD IN DUBAI

LESBIANS SENTENCED TO MONTH IN JAIL FOR
KISSING ON DUBAI BEACH

This punitive approach is very much at odds with the image the city projects to the outside world: a fun-filled liberal playground where the party never stops. And contrasted with the severe sentences given for drug-related offenses, there have been some head-scratching punishments handed down for others:

SIX MONTHS' JAIL FOR "DAYDREAMER" WHO KILLED
TRAFFIC POLICEMAN

POLICEMAN RECEIVES [ONE YEAR] JAIL SENTENCE
AFTER MOLESTING GIRL IN BACKSEAT OF CAR

BROTHERS GET [THREE YEAR] JAIL TERMS FOR
ABUSING TEENAGERS AND RAPING THEIR FRIEND

THREE YEARS FOR TORTURING HOUSEMAID USING
ABU GHRAIB-STYLE PRISON TORTURE TACTICS

DRUNK DRIVER KILLER TO SPEND ONE YEAR IN JAIL

Dubai's criminal justice system does not follow a western rulebook. Probably its greatest idiosyncrasy is the selective and adjustable application of the rule of law. Dubai can always make an exception to any rule, as long as it is prudent to do so.

When an American music producer was arrested for cocaine possession at the airport en route to a celebrity bash at the Burj Al Arab, he inadvertently became the poster child for Dubai's binary approach to drug enforcement. Luckily for Dallas Austin, he was not only rich, he also had famous friends. And if there is one thing the powers that be understand and value, it is the power of celebrity to push the dream they are selling. After a US Senator and Lionel Richie both intervened on his behalf, Mr. Austin was brought to trial. He was duly convicted and sentenced to the mandatory four-year stretch, but immediately received a royal pardon and was flown out of the country a few hours later. Sweet justice indeed.

Although the authorities are loath to admit it, there was one factor that probably increased Austin's chances of being stopped and searched at Dubai International Airport: he is black. From my own statistically meaningless enquiries, I suspect that Dubai's customs officials have been issued with a long checklist from which they can identify your quintessential recreational drug user. Without going into details, if you are a long-haired man of color with visible tattoos and body piercings, I advise against transiting through Dubai on your way back from that reggae festival in Amsterdam. But in Mr. Austin's case, there was never going to be any other verdict. It was by harnessing the power associated with celebrity and wealth that Dubai managed to turn itself into a global brand. Dumping a big pile of sand into the sea has only limited news value (even if it is the biggest pile of sand ever!) unless you attach a famous face like Tiger Woods or Michael Schumacher to the project. Celebrities wouldn't be in such a rush to Dubai if one of their own was languishing in jail just for having a little bit of blow in his pocket. Allowances are made accordingly.

However, the vagaries of the legal system don't stop there. There are also multiple applications of the law depending on which rung of the social ladder you call home. There's one interpretation if you're local, rich, and/or well connected; another for celebrities stopping off to promote Dubai as a global center of unabashed merriment; a further set of rules to follow if you're an Average Joe Emirati; followed by another if you're a middle-class expatriate or business owner. Further down the food chain things get more opaque. Even when driving, speed limits and other rules of the road are of concern to most but not all of the groups mentioned above.

The real difficulty arises in finding out which of the emirate's laws really apply you. For example, an unmarried woman from the US should be able to cohabit or have consensual sex with an unmarried man from England without any problems, even though this is technically deemed adultery and is a criminal offense. If one of those involved is a Muslim, Arab, or local (or maybe all three), they had better be more careful. When trouble does arise, an "adulterer" may face the wrath of the law because a spurned lover or enemy has filed a complaint; as a rule, the police don't go knocking on bedroom doors. An Englishwoman received a custodial sentence for "adultery" when her ex-husband (an Egyptian) filed a complaint that she was alone in her house with a man to whom she was not married.

The lessons to be learned from all this are nuanced, but essentially simple. Despite the coffee shops and the sushi bars, despite the beaches and the nightclubs, when a westerner disembarks at DXB, it is important to bear in mind that you are not in Kansas any more.

If you need stronger evidence regarding the legal differences at work, you only have to go back to the 1930s, when justice was dispensed in an even more capricious fashion. After a mini-revolt against the ruling family was suppressed, some of the rebels were punished in a manner that almost defies description. A letter I came across in the archives of the Political Resident (courtesy of the Juma Al Majed library) still has the power to unsettle today:

The Event of Ramadhan Night or Present-time Savagery.
The "AL BAHRAIN" newspaper already published this news of the betrayal of Said bin Maktoum to his cousins, murder of Shaikh Bashar bin Rashid on 7th Safar 1358 and the loss of the lives of innocent persons who were killed at the Customs House at Dairah for no fault on their part...

On the day of the massacre, Kalifa bin Said [the brother of Sheikh Rashid] attacked the customs house and said, "I have been instructed to take you to prison and you need not be afraid..."

His brother Rashid... by his orders fire was set to blaze on which iron nails were placed until they became red hot. Then several men sat on the breast of those persons one by one and another man came and thrust the iron nail in their eyes very severely. With this they were not even satisfied. They began testing their eyesight by applying torch light to them and asking them whether they could see or not. They were then left alone in their fetters. Next morning, they released them from prison and asked them to go to their houses without any guide and without being carried by some means. They entered the market blindly and in a highly lamentable condition. By doing so they intended to give a lesson to the people but, on the contrary, their action was received by indignation.

For the benefit of history and truth please publish this article in the first issue of your newspaper.

Khalid al Fahad

It is worth noting that other researchers have attested that a liquid was used instead of an iron nail and that the unlucky victims only had one eye blinded. The letter ended with a note from the British Political Resident. He believed that the writer had used a false name, obviously in fear of being subjected to the same "pluck out his eyes, apologize" approach to penal correction.

The tradition of preferring anonymity to openness continues to this day. Journalists in Dubai are often reluctant to speak unfettered, even if the penalties for upsetting the authorities are nowhere near as severe as in the past. Human nature being what it is, however, there are always some people who just can't stay silent. Thus Dubai's information gap is frequently filled not on television or in newsprint, but by a vibrant, caustic, and occasionally inflammatory community of bloggers, sometimes the only source of unrestrained comment you can find.

One of Dubai's most outspoken (and anonymous) bloggers agreed to come out of the closet. After an exchange of emails, my meeting with Secret Dubai Diary (hereafter

known as SD) was set for a coffee shop in the Mall of the
Emirates, a suitable location for the voice of Dubai's new
generation of expatriates. It was only while on my way to
meet SD that a light bulb went on in my head. I didn't
know the name, age, gender, or nationality of this undercover blogger. Sadly, a text message clarifying those aforementioned particulars ended my fantasies of a clandestine
rendezvous, rife with Cold War intrigue.

SD turned out to be a young British woman. A journalist, she had come to Dubai for "the adventure, the experience, the travel and because of an interesting and
challenging new job." Initially she had fallen for its
charms, but the romance didn't last. "Dubai changed
greatly from when I arrived to what it is now. They are
making some strides in education, women's rights, transport, but certain things lost their gloss and the negative elements, like the appalling and unsustainable development,
started to jar more," she said.

I wanted to talk to SD about Dubai's penchant for
blocking websites and trying to silence blogs such as her
own. Recently a ban had been slapped on an online jour-
nal supposedly written by two Arab women, who blogged
in salacious detail about their sexcapades around the city.
"Dubai is full of prostitutes, yet two women talking about
consensual sex is deemed inappropriate!" SD said. She
believed that the key factor in the decision to block the site
was the fact that the women in question claimed to be
Arab, even though some of their *double entendres* sounded
a little British to her ears.

SD had also raised the ire of the authorities. Her own
blog had been blocked, unblocked, and then blocked
again. Some locals had organized an online campaign to
have her website banned after taking offense to a satirical
poem (written by someone else) that she had posted on her

site. But she wasn't that concerned: "The first block didn't stop me posting before, and it won't stop me posting this time. When I was unblocked I felt this kind of weighty responsibility to be more polite. Now [after being blocked again] I don't have that burden and I don't want it back!" This propensity to censure free speech didn't impress her and she felt that Dubai's claim to be one of the world's leading cities was overstepping the mark somewhat: "You can't get away with this kind of oppression and human rights abuses if you want to put yourself up against London and New York. You have to open up, grow up, and actually develop your nation, not paint a thin, glossy skin over a festering boil of third world-style dictatorship."

Professionally she had also encountered difficulties, even during the course of writing seemingly innocuous articles. One feature on the influence of Bedouin culture on modern-day Saudi Arabia was killed by the Arab editorial team with the following justification: Saudis do not want to be associated with the desert. For someone who had chosen the media as a career, the self-censorship practiced by so many journalists felt oppressive. "Dubai's media is immensely backward for the type of country it claims to be. Sure, progress has been made, but not nearly enough. Compared to the average dictatorship-style regime, it's probably no better and no worse than many. Better than North Korea, worse than Singapore. But it is hard to compare because different regimes censor different kinds of things," she added.

Despite these censorious tendencies, it must be said that media professionals in Dubai do not share the same concerns as their colleagues in Iran, Syria, or Iraq. They don't live in fear of late-night visits from the *mukharabat* (secret police) or sectarian death squads. The dread Dubai generates among its newsmen and women is generally financial. Fines rather than imprisonment are the penalties that await newspapers and journalists for opaque offenses such as "criticizing the head of state, damaging the economy or insulting local traditions." Self-censorship is generally how things work. Editors are afraid of getting fired by newspaper owners, while journalists fear getting the sack from their editors. If you are British, losing your job could involve a hasty retreat to the UK, accompanied by a significant decrease in your standard of living. For an Arab or Indian journalist, a return to their homeland would involve a more drastic reduction in remuneration – money that can support a large extended family back home. And if a journalist comes from the Philippines, Iraq, or Lebanon, going home implies a significant increase in personal danger, large numbers of their colleagues being killed or imprisoned each year. Overall, it's best to keep quiet.

In any case, even the media laws operate under a two-tier system. The international news outlets operating in Media City are exempt from many of the regulations under which local news organizations must work. As such, local newspapers are often seen as mere mouthpieces of the government, as the public know that this is all that the authorities will tolerate. All this may explain why the word *sahafa* (journalist) is often viewed as a dirty word in much of the Gulf. In such an environment, Dubai is often seen as the place where western journalists go to die, metaphorically speaking of course. Given the choice between tackling controversial news stories that might jeopardize their golf club membership and their children's international school, most gentlemen of the press who relocate from the West realize that discretion is the better part of valor. They learn to be content with the glossy features and feel-good stories that the authorities (and their editors) like to read.

SD understood why many people working in Dubai took the easy option, but she had no time for those who tried to defend themselves from a professional point of view: "That is fine so long as they are aware of what they are doing. But when they try to start justifying it or become apologists for the censorship, that's when they're a damn disgrace to journalism. At that stage they should leave and go into government PR."

For those journalists who decide to stay, television shows such as *Emirates News* form one such career option – a place where the distinction between public relations and news fades to gray. *Emirates News* is in many ways the perfect embodiment of Brand Dubai: a shiny but often vacuous enterprise, whose main purpose in life is to promote the city rather than report the news. *Emirates News* is the place where state-controlled media, public relations, marketing, and reportage meet, court, and couple before giving birth to a journalistic chimera.

Admittedly summer is the silly season for news, but the selection of stories on *Emirates News* one night left me gobsmacked. The lead story focused on the need for shaded bus shelters to shield commuters from the sun. This was followed by the obligatory bit of royal hagiography common in every Gulf state: "His Highness Sheikh So-and-So, in the presence of His Highness Sheikh So-and-So, today oversaw plans for the construction of an extension to the Municipal Zoo," or words to that effect. Another story focused on the Dubai Chamber of Commerce's new business directory. The newscaster announced to the world that the various companies would be listed (wait for it) in alphabetical order! This breakthrough was followed by the exact number of new entries that had been added to the tome that year. The precise figure was either 12,206 or 12,602. After the break, there was a feature story on the

South African tourist industry. The text read like a press release (from the South African tourist board, perhaps?) and was read over video footage I'm convinced was also supplied by the tourist board. Across the Middle East, both private and state-run news organizations are often run this way, reprinting or rehashing the same mix of government statements and corporate press releases, often to an unsuspecting public. But the night's broadcast ended in truly spectacular fashion with a postmodernist flourish: a news story on Dubai television about the increasing number of news stories about Dubai on television stations outside of Dubai. Marshall McLuhan and Jean Baudrillard would both have been so proud.

14

First Among Equals

WHAT COUNTRY WAS I IN – the United Arab Emirates or Oman? For the last few minutes my mobile phone had been peppered with incoming text messages, welcoming me to the Sultanate of Oman and then back to the UAE. Despite the territorial changes, the scenery hadn't changed and I hadn't seen a border checkpoint. My map wasn't much help either. All I could make out were a series of concentric circles tightly wound together trying to separate the two countries. It was all very confusing. The demarcation lines that exist within the UAE are not for the faint hearted. A cursory glance reveals seven brides for seven brothers. Each of the country's seven emirates – Abu Dhabi, Dubai, Sharjah, Ajman, Um Al Quwain, Ras Al Khaimah, and Fujerah – constitutes both a city and a province, with their own clearly delimited borders. But a closer examination reveals other cartographical anomalies.

The mountain villages in the eastern part of the country have always had an identity crisis. Far away from the bright lights of Dubai, in the mountainous east of the UAE, is the little mountain village of Hatta. Although an hour's drive from where the emirate's territorial jurisdiction seems to end, Hatta is clearly marked on every map as belonging to Dubai. A jaunt there is a very common day trip from Dubai, even if the road takes you through the exclaves of two other emirates (Sharjah and Ajman), with a detour into the neighboring country of Oman for good measure.

The odd delimitations that exist within the federation are a legacy of the days when much of the western littoral of the Persian Gulf (referred to as either the Trucial States or Trucial Oman) was administered en masse by the British. With the passing of empire and the onset of independence, this loose gathering of tribes and sheikhdoms had to be broken up. The British had already seen the result of their handiwork in India (an estimated one million dead after partition) and probably didn't want a repeat performance. A federation was needed to keep the peace, but the territory of each sheikh and the tribes within it would have to be carefully defined if peace was to hold. (Bahrain and Qatar were initially invited to join the UAE but RSVP-ed in the negative and opted for independence in their own right.) New borders were needed. Thus it is in the mountains in the east of the country that you can find some of the most idiosyncratic lines in the sand ever to be etched by a departing colonial power.

A troupe of diplomats and cartographers were dispatched to conjure a nation state from the tribal protectorates along the Trucial Coast. In the build-up to independence, representatives of the Crown were sent to the Hajar Mountains tasked with determining the loyalties of the various tribes who lived there. My favorite version of the story involves a man on a camel roaming from village to village, determining to which of the coastal sheikhs each mountain clan pledged fealty – which was by no means written in stone. Loyalty was bargained for and could be bought. Ibn Saud, the founder of Saudi Arabia, once tried to convince the inhabitants of the Burami oasis in present-day Abu Dhabi to switch their allegiance to him by sending in a representative to hand out money and cook large meals for the local population – and it almost worked. Anyway, after plotting the coordinates of each village on a map and joining the dots back in London, the boundaries of the emirates in the soon-to-be-formed United Arab Emirates were drawn accordingly. While the British have

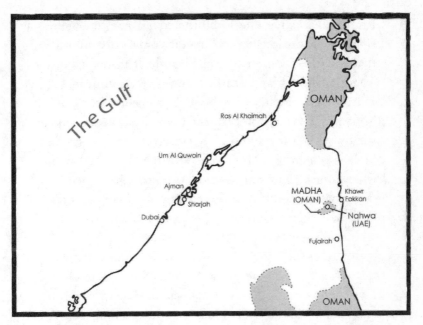

received unending criticism for the wanton ethnic-sundering lines they drew across the sands of the Middle East and Africa in the past, one can only admire the micro-managed display of cartography that willed into being the faint spot on the map that is the tiny enclave of Nahwa.

After the negotiations that led to the 1971 declaration of independence, a little circle of land belonging to Oman (known as Madha) was left marooned within the UAE. However, within this tiny piece of Oman, there were a few families loyal to the Sheikh of Sharjah who didn't want to be Omanis. Potentially a problem, all it took was a quick flick of a pencil and the crisis was solved. Another circle was drawn within Oman and an enclave belonging to the UAE was willed into being. This little loop of land is called Nahwa and could be seen as the most inspired piece of diplomacy of Britain's 400-year history in Arabia.

I had set out for Nahwa earlier that morning after spending the previous night in the eastern coastal town of

Khor Fakkan. I had checked into a hotel under the impression that I was lodging in Fujairah, only to be informed that the hotel was actually in Sharjah. It turns out there were tranches of land nearby administered jointly by both Fujairah and Sharjah – obviously some of those questioned by the man on his camel couldn't make up their minds. As I drove south along the coast road, a grumpy Gulf of Oman proved no match for the Hajar Mountains when competing for my attention. Even with an incoming *shamal* wind kicking dust up into the air, these mountains are spectacular, imposing upsurges of black basalt rock with claret veins weaved into the surface.

Soon after turning off the main road, and without my knowledge, I made the transition from the UAE to Oman. I was only certain about the change once the white, green, and red bars of the Omani flag with the traditional curved *khanjar* dagger in front of two crossed swords appeared, flying over a school. Across the Gulf, Oman is noted for being rather well kept. The ruling Sultan is reputed to have ordered all window AC units to be covered with stylish trellises in a bid to keep up appearances. And here in this little Omani enclave of Madha, the water tanks on top of the houses were shaped like a fort's battlements.

After only a few minutes, my sojourn in Oman was over and the red, green, white, and black flag of the UAE reappeared, flying high over the police outpost of Nahwa. I was in the enclave inside the enclave. An English friend who has spent a good deal of time exploring the great outdoors of the Arabian Peninsula was the inspiration for my next move. He insists that border guards and policemen in such remote places are more than happy to receive visitors and often prove to be excellent hosts. Whereas the borders drawn by the former imperial powers in other parts of the Middle East (Israel and Lebanon for example) demand significantly more vigilance, similar outposts in the more remote areas of Gulf countries engender considerably less paranoia. Thus, as I walked in the front door of the police station unannounced, it wasn't a great surprise to be greeted cheerfully by two policemen sitting down to a large breakfast. They invited me to join them. After polishing off a full repast of salted tuna, lentils, fava beans, and pita bread, we talked for a while. The larger of the two men told me about training courses he had taken in the US and described the invigorative effects of the fish we had just eaten.

An hour later I was back on the road. The asphalt came to an end not far past the police station and from there I continued on foot. I walked along a steep-sided *wadi* (dry river bed) that sliced through the landscape, cascading through the rock from the higher ground above. The rocky floor was strewn with boulders, which tumble down the mountainside each year as flash floods sweep through the valleys. As the morning sun attempted to break through the haze overhead, I was engulfed by a sense of serenity and calmness. In other parts of the Middle East that day, people would awake to headlines filled with death, destruction, and hatred; a violence that is all the more contemptible given its predictability, a bloodshed that is all the more tragic given that it has become a part of everyday life. Communities across the region in Lebanon, Syria, Palestine, Israel, and Iraq are destined to relive the horrors of their history each day, fueled in no small part by lines etched in the sands many years before. But here, with the sun now shining brightly and the wind rustling through the air, Nahwa felt like the most peaceful place on earth. Maybe the man on the camel got a few things right after all.

The young man from Abu Dhabi was clearly upset. I could understand his frustration. "Everyone thinks Dubai is the capital of UAE! If we go outside our country and people ask us where we are from, when we say Abu Dhabi, they don't know it. Some people don't even know the UAE. They say, 'Where is this?' But when we say Dubai, then everybody knows! They think Dubai is the capital of the UAE, some people think Dubai is a country!" he said.

I had met Fahad while walking through Dubai's Heritage Village, a mini-theme park dedicated to Ye Olde Dubai located alongside the Creek. Here, a selection of traditional foods was being prepared by local Emirati women, all wearing the *burqa* and chatting to each other. It was while talking to one of these older women (she wanted to know which character from the television show *Freej* looked most like her) that Fahad and his friends overheard my attempts to murder their native language. Yet even the most basic deployment of Arabic engenders joy in the Gulf, and I was immediately invited to join them for an impromptu al fresco supper.

In their mid-twenties, they were in Dubai for a training course; they only got to go back home to Abu Dhabi at the weekends. Their feelings toward Dubai were ambivalent at best. No one likes to be overshadowed, particularly by a sibling. It is in just such a spirit that generations of young Canadians and Kiwis have headed off around the world with maple leaves and ferns sewn onto their backpacks, loath to be mistaken for either Americans or Australians. Even though Abu Dhabi is both the biggest and by far the wealthiest of all the emirates within the UAE, there is no doubting that it has been vastly outshone by its kid brother. According to these young men, Dubai had got "a little too big for its spats."

For the sake of appearances, the United Arab Emirates is officially a democratic federation governed by a Supreme

Council, which consists of the head of each of the seven emirates. And though the British exerted a great deal of effort to give all the emirates a voice in the new federation, in reality the UAE has always been a two-man show. This has been the way ever since Sheikh Rashid of Dubai and Sheikh Zayed of Abu Dhabi met on the border of their respective principalities in 1968 and agreed that a union needed to be formed. After some lingering border disputes had been settled, the other emirates were invited to make up the numbers. Abu Dhabi became the capital city and the ruler of Abu Dhabi (by far the wealthiest emirate due to its oil reserves) was to act as the perpetual President of the UAE, while the ruler of Dubai would become the Vice-President. In reality, these terms bear little resemblance to the posts that exist in your average western democracy.

Their intra-territorial boundaries established, the constituent members of the newly formed United Arab Emirates were then able to take their first steps as part of the international community. This union was undertaken in a profusion of "benevolent brotherly relations" and "friendly fraternal feelings"; diplomatic language in the Gulf, just like the tea, can be exceptionally syrupy. The new country was nothing if not optimistic and Article 14 of the constitution outlined a somewhat utopian vision of the future:

> *Society shall be based, inter alia, on equality, social justice, security, peace and equal opportunities for all citizens, who shall be bound together by the strongest ties of solidarity, mutual love and understanding.*

Yet less than quarter of a century before the constitution was inked, Dubai and Abu Dhabi were on less than cordial terms. In many parts of the Gulf, past disputes are often more ignored than forgiven and simply whitewashed from the history books. To get an unedited (though not necessarily impartial) view of past events, you are generally forced to dig a little deeper than official histories. While browsing through an archive of official correspondence of former Political Residents (here again the Jumah Al Majed library proved invaluable), I came across some communiqués that shed light on the testy relationship between Abu Dhabi and Dubai during the time Thesiger traveled through the region. A Mr. M Jackman (Political Agent, Bahrain) was addressing Lt. Col. A.C. Galloway (Political Resident in the Persian Gulf) concerning ongoing troubles between Dubai and its neighbor to the west:

> *The Shaikh of Dubai has now reported that on the 28th August a party consisting of three Abu Dhabi subjects and two Awamir tribesmen stole 20 Dubai camels from the vicinity of Jabal Ali; that on the 1st September six Abu Dhabi subjects raided Muwaih Abyadh and took away 18 camels; and that on the 7th September a third raiding party consisting of 70 Manasir tribesmen stole about 200 camels. Two Dubai subjects were killed and one wounded in the last raid. It is alleged by Dubai that most of the thieves are in the employ of Shaikh Shakbut [Ruler of Abu Dhabi], who has supplied the raiders with arms in the hope of compelling Dubai to make peace with his former allies direct.*

This kind of activity inevitably caused tension between Dubai and Abu Dhabi. Both rulers sometimes had to assume the role of a concerned parent summoned by the school principal (in this case the British Political Resident) to account for the actions of a tearaway child (the desert tribes they were supposed to control). Mr. Jackman's letter was dated 1947. Just after the Second World War had inflicted industrial-scale destruction across Europe and the Far East, Dubai and Abu Dhabi were involved in disputes over livestock.

By the 1960s, when the Trucial Coast was still finalizing tribal loyalties and boundaries, the rest of the Middle East was experiencing wider regional conflicts that made these disputes seem rather insignificant. With the Cold War being fought by proxy in their backyard (Israel had the US in its corner while the USSR was the "cut man" for Syria and Egypt), the local sheikhs realized there were far bigger "raiders" to be afraid of. In the interest of survival Dubai and Abu Dhabi buried the hatchet, but thankfully not in each other. Previous disputes were set aside and, like the *hajj* caravans of yesteryear, strength was found in numbers. Officially, these past disputes are now forgotten. And if there are any lingering animosities, they certainly won't be aired on December 2 each year, when the UAE celebrates its National Day. A certain amount of collective amnesia is a must if a nation is ever going to progress.

Once we had eaten, Fahad and my new-found companions offered to take me on a tour of the city. After viewing some of the sights and drinking milky tea flavored with saffron outside a suburban café, we finished off the evening in a pool hall. Although they were dressed traditionally in *kanduras* and *gutras*, they were perfectly at ease amid the Lebanese, Filipinos, Indians, and English people wiling away a hot summer night. Despite the fact that many of the outer trappings of the traditional society that Thesiger witnessed have disappeared from Arabia, these young men had not simply abandoned their past.

In Thesiger's *Arabian Sands*, the specter of modernization and the inevitable change it would bring for the local people always hovers in the background. Yet as I looked around the pool table, there was still a cultural continuity in evidence that would not simply disappear. Most of these men had kept to their local traditions by marrying young, and many already had children of their own. Those who smoked eschewed cigarettes; they preferred the small, thin pipe that is the traditional form of tobacco ingestion. And above all, they couldn't wait till their training course was over so that they could move back home to Abu Dhabi. They preferred to spend their free time in the desert or on their farms, away from the bright lights and traffic. They couldn't wait to leave all this behind and, by extension, the plantation of an alien world in their homeland. But at the same time, they also knew why foreigners liked Dubai so much. "It is free," Fahad said. As we said our goodbyes at the end of the evening, their native pride resurfaced. Fahad insisted that if I wanted to experience true Arabian hospitality, I would have to visit his home town.

Sometime later I followed Fahad's advice and took the road west to the UAE's largest emirate. Abu Dhabi literally means "father of the gazelle." The legend that surrounds the founding of the city involves a hunting party tracking a gazelle all the way from Liwa to the coast. The hunters liked what they saw. Initially, Abu Dhabi served as a summer residence for pearl diving, but it slowly gained in importance: it was the discovery of oil that made Abu Dhabi the first among equals that it is today.

Given the impact of the man, it is fitting that the first structure of note a visitor sees driving into Abu Dhabi is the imposing Sheikh Zayed Al Nahyan Mosque. Built in the Moghul style, this mass of white marble is named after the "father of the nation," the man who put the "united" in the United Arab Emirates. Sheikh Zayed ruled Abu Dhabi from 1966 until his death in 2004 and became the first president of the UAE after independence. In keeping with the fact that he was one of the richest men in the world (due to the Nahyan family's personal control of Abu Dhabi's oil reserves), he was laid to rest in the world's third/fourth/fifth biggest mosque, depending on who's doing the arithmetic. The mosque is home to a number of world records – the world's largest Persian carpet and chandelier are just two of its claims to fame. Dubai does not enjoy a monopoly on gigantism.

When compared to Dubai, Abu Dhabi is certainly in a different weight class when it comes to raw punching power. Accounting for nearly 90 percent of the UAE's land area and sitting on nearly 10 percent of the world's proven oil reserves, Abu Dhabi is milking a cash cow of mammoth proportions. In 2008, its GDP hit US$105 billion after pumping some 2.7 million barrels of oil a day at up to US$147 per barrel. Some elementary mathematics tells you that liquidity is not a major problem for this emirate. In Abu Dhabi, oil accounts for over 90 percent of government revenue. In Dubai, the figure is only around 5 percent. Furthermore, Abu Dhabi has stockpiled several hundred billion dollars abroad in a diverse portfolio of investments that should see it through any leaner times.

Given this vast oil wealth, Abu Dhabi is not dependent on trade and has never felt the pressing need to develop an open economy or actively embrace or empower the foreigners living there. Dubai, on the other hand, even has fully enclosed air-conditioned bus stops for its expats. In the rest of the Gulf, such a proposal would be laughable. As only poor foreigners take public transport, why bother making it comfortable?

My first hint that Abu Dhabi was not the multicultural love-in of Dubai came just outside Abu Dhabi itself via that time-honored journalistic source: graffiti on the back of a door of a men's toilet at a petrol station. A running conversation had been taking a place for some time between two anonymous scribes.

"I am local boy, I love big dick," was the first contribution, which was followed by two other exhortations written in the same hand.

"Love Arabic."

"Fuck Arabic."

The response was short and to the point: "Fuck you. Fuck you all Phaillabiono."

Exactly how the second writer knew that the first was from the Philippines, I couldn't tell. And the second had followed up with a closing comment reaffirming his position: "Phallopin focker."

Given the fact that the second writer had misspelled the same word in two different ways and the general confusion between *b* and *p*, my experience as a teacher of English led me to suspect that the penmanship belonged to someone whose first language was Arabic. These penciled messages in a public convenience had obviously struck a nerve with the passing pissing populace. A host of others had also joined in this frank exchange of ideas. In doing so, they had created a low-tech version of the discussion threads you find on Secret Dubai's blog. Out of the various claims and counterclaims scribbled all over the door, one piece of advice stood out. This was an astute recommendation that all long-term expats who live in the Gulf (and anywhere else for that matter) should bear in mind: "If you don't like them go back home fucker."

A clearer picture of the position foreigners occupy in Abu Dhabi's social order was revealed in a scandal involving the brother of the Abu Dhabi crown prince. After supposedly being cheated out of a truckload of grain by an

Afghan merchant, the sheikh set about torturing the unfortunate man (with the aid of a uniformed policeman) while recording his retribution on video for posterity. The abuse inflicted on his victim included (among other things) beating him with a stick spiked with nails, then literally pouring salt on his wounds, before finally driving over the poor man repeatedly in his Mercedes SUV. When pressed on the issue, the Ministry of Justice in Abu Dhabi issued a statement that the matter had been "settled privately" and that the sheikh's actions were not part of a "pattern of behavior."

The second building that caught my eye was a shop called the Yugoslavian Furniture Company; an indication that Abu Dhabi doesn't move with the times at quite the same speed as Dubai. Then again, it doesn't really have to. Abu Dhabi's oil revenues are so bloated it has earned the title "the richest city in the world," and there are only a tiny number of locals between which to divvy up the billions earned each year.

A friend who worked in the oil industry was my host for the evening. Along with showing me some of the haunts popular with western expatriates, he also dissected the various tribal divisions within the city's Pathan population with the help of a talkative Pakistani taxi driver. Working for an oil company comes with nice perks: the tax-free salaries are generous and you can still clock off around 3 o'clock in the afternoon. There is also a British club for those in need of a pint of nostalgia. As such, Abu Dhabi retains some of the sleepy old-world charm expatriates remember from the 1970s, though this is even more the case in Al Ain, the emirate's second city. Overall, though, entertainment options in Abu Dhabi are limited and lack a little vigor (despite the licentious attractions of the Ali Pally Hotel).

But Abu Dhabi had grown tired of Dubai grabbing all the headlines and set about upping its brand recognition the way it knows best: by shoveling out bucketfuls of cash. A number of major donations convinced both the Guggenheim Museum and the Louvre to open franchises in Abu Dhabi. The plan was to turn it into a "cappuccino" tourist destination as opposed to the "instant" served up in Dubai. Another building that sought to redress Abu Dhabi's lack of international presence was the US$3 billion Emirates Palace Hotel, supposedly "the most expensive hotel in the world." The afternoon I stopped in for lunch, I was impressed by the craftsmanship – the hotel is a marble and gold fest second to none. My meal was good, but the repressed restaurant critic inside me still found the tiniest of black marks for my review: the salt and pepper shakers were the wrong way around. The salt shaker had multiple holes while the pepper shaker had one. An insignificant point perhaps, yet as I looked around at the lavish surroundings, it encapsulated the essential difference between Dubai and its oil-rich big brother.

Abu Dhabi had built the world's most expensive hotel, but it still did not enjoy the iconic status enjoyed by the Burj Al Arab. And when it comes to entertaining foreigners, Dubai tries to be highly customer oriented. Abu Dhabi is not so accommodating and for me, it all came back to basics like salt and pepper. I doubted that this inversion of the condiments was some important cultural tradition the hotel's management was keen to maintain, so why didn't somebody fix it? Was it simply a lack of awareness? Could it be that after spending so many billions on the hotel, the management decided to skimp on the staff? The one thing Dubai understands is that if you want to provide "world-class" service, you need people who at least understand what that concept actually means. Or it could simply be that the management was afraid a VIP would get royally pissed off if he accidentally shook a load of pepper on his chips.

There was also a certain lack of imagination in Abu Dhabi's attempt to rebrand itself. When Dubai sponsored an English football team, Abu Dhabi decided it had to buy one. Abu Dhabi has also established a state-funded airline along the lines of Dubai's Emirates Airways; while the global airline industry was rushing for greater consolidation, it was telling that the UAE (with its tiny population) now had two rival "national" carriers. The old propensities toward independence and competition die hard. This sibling rivalry has been characterized by many analogies. One journalist used a 1950s comparison, styling Dubai as a voluptuous Marilyn Monroe and Abu Dhabi as a more refined Grace Kelly. My own preferred parallel is an Arabian equivalent of the Rumble in the Jungle: Abu Dhabi in one corner as a muscular yet lumbering George Foreman, Dubai in the other as a sassy, brash, jive-talking Muhammad Ali, riding its luck while defying both perceived wisdom and the prophets of doom.

It took a collapse in global credit markets to bring Dubai down to size and reaffirm Abu Dhabi's position as the "first among equals" in the UAE. The Dubai dream was carried along on a tidal wave of cheap credit and excess liquidity: billions of borrowed dollars were plowed into a decade-long building boom. When the subsequent property bubble finally popped, Dubai was shown to be "all prick and no pence" and was forced to go cap in hand to Abu Dhabi for a "dig out." The UAE Central Bank (that is, Abu Dhabi) agreed to purchase several billion dollars worth of "Dubai Bonds" to prop up its neighbor as it attempted to ride out the crunch. Its high-flying sibling had been humbled.

Though Dubai had experienced economic hardship before – the pearling industry collapsed in the 1930s leaving many destitute – these twenty-first-century injuries were self-inflicted. Dubai had effectively bankrupted itself. When Dubai World – the largest branch of Maktoum Inc. – was forced to "restructure" debt repayments of some US$60 billion, the analogy with Mohammed Ali resonated even further. The Champ, like Dubai, had touted himself unabashedly as "the Greatest" to anyone who would listen. And while his performances were the stuff of legend, ultimately he didn't know when to stop and ended up doing serious damage to himself.

For Dubai's less hallowed residents, there were more pressing, more mundane predicaments. The construction workers who had built the dream were the first to feel the pain. When they lost their jobs a costly return home lay ahead, with neither the gold nor the cash they had expected to accumulate. Expats who had plowed all their money into the booming property market saw the value of their investments fall through the floor; others who had lost their jobs and were unable to pay their bills fled the country in fear of ending up in debtors' prison, abandoning their cars at the airport with notes inside apologizing for any inconvenience caused. While Sheikh Mohammed protested that Dubai was "strong and persistent" and that only "the fruit-bearing tree... becomes the target of [stone] throwers," a previous epigram of his also seemed apropos given his choice of financial advisers during the boom times: "Take wisdom from the wise – not everyone who rides is a jockey."

Along with this loss of prestige, history suggests that failing to manage the public purse can also result in an erosion of political power. During the first big oil boom in the 1970s, the oil-rich Gulf states went on an unmerciful decade-long bender (and not always in the metaphorical sense) with much of their oil revenues, investing in a number of dubious projects both at home and abroad. The hangover kicked in around 1982, when Kuwait's Souk Al Manakh (an unofficial stock market that ended up as a gigantic Ponzi scheme) imploded, leaving a US$90 billion hole in the regional economy. While Kuwait's ruling Al Sabah family oversaw an economy with enough oil reserves to organize a bailout, analysts have identified this as a turning point for the country's nascent democracy movement. Since the Souk Al Manakh crash, the ability of the Al Sabah family to act unilaterally has been noticeably curtailed, as the country's hitherto placid parliament transformed into the region's most vociferous and cantankerous law-making body.

Whatever the future may have in store for Maktoum Inc, one outcome at least was a certainty. After the latest cycle of boom and bust to come waltzing through the region, it was Dubai's turn to wake up the morning after more than a little the worse for wear.

15

She Sells Sanctuary

Arabia Felix! Strange that the epithet "Happy" should grace a part of the earth's surface, most of it barren wilderness where, since the dawn of history, man has ever been at war with his environment and his neighbour.

Bertram Thomas (1931)

WHEN THE CLASSICAL GEOGRAPHER PTOLEMY coined the phrase *Eudaimon Arabia* (happy or fortunate Arabia) some 3,000 years ago, it was the frankincense and myrrh that oozed from the trees of Yemen and Oman that set his descriptive juices flowing. Worth their weight in gold, these aromatic gums were used in temples when invoking the pantheon of Greek gods. A civilization later, when the Roman Emperor Augustus ordered a doomed army into the deserts of the Arabian Peninsula (by then it had acquired the catchier Latin handle *Arabia Felix*), he too was motivated by a covetous desire for the same natural resources.

In the twentieth century, the desire for frankincense and myrrh was replaced by a lust for another unctuous substance. Oil has fueled the fires of conflict across much of the Arab world for the last 50 years. But while petroleum has brought good fortune to many, its mishandling has also been a source of untold misfortune for others. Across the Middle East, oil has sustained both the egoism of dictators and the blind belief of zealots. It has driven nations to war, sundered families, and sent untold thousands into exile. For those forced to flee their homes in search of a Middle East sanctuary, Dubai is often the first port of call.

The coffee shop in Satwa was full of one such band of exiles: Iraqis who had fled the security situation (or the absence thereof) back home after the US invasion and the toppling of Saddam Hussein. But today there were more important affairs of state to attend to – the Iraqi football team was playing Saudi Arabia in the final of the Asia Cup. Although Iraqis have earned a reputation in some quarters for being fond of a scrap, these football fans were impeccably behaved, smoking coiled *shisha* pipes and sipping glasses of mint tea. The languid reclining normally associated with the Arabian tea house – bodies stretched across sofas propped up on bolsters and cushions – had given way to edge-of-the-seat foot tapping and a maelstrom of curses and exaltations over disputed calls and near misses.

Sitting beside me was Khamees, one of only three local men in the café. Though the Iraqi team (who couldn't even train in their own country) had generated a lot of public sympathy, Khamees was firmly behind Saudi Arabia. "Just don't tell these people," he whispered jokingly, completely outnumbered by the fifty or so Iraqis glued to the television. In this case, the demographics were almost correct. While exact numbers are hard to pin down, locals such as Khamees make up about 5 percent of Dubai's population. Accounting for about 80,000 people out of a population of approximately two million, locals must become accustomed to being outnumbered from an early age.

At half-time the score was 0–0. While the Iraqi fans took a much-needed break, Khamees and I got to talking about the future of UAE football. The UAE had won the Gulf Cup just that year, so there had been expectations that the team might make some progress on a wider stage.

But Khamees wasn't that impressed with the players since then. "After they won the Gulf Cup, they got money and watches from the government, but then they did nothing!" he said, his displeasure clearly evident. I was expecting this outburst to be followed by a paean to the glory days of amateurism, when men played for the love of the game and pride in the shirt. However, Khamees had a different solution to his national team's recent drop in form: "They should pay to bring foreign players from outside, like in Qatar."

He was referring to the contentious approach taken by Dubai's Gulf neighbor to achieve recognition in the sporting arena. In the search for sporting success, the Qatari authorities had begun handing out passports to a horde of gallowglasses from across the world of athletics. All an athlete had to do was take an Arab/Muslim name, trouser the cash on offer, and don the purple tracksuit of Qatar at the next Olympiad. So it came to pass that a nation that had never previously troubled the scorer at international athletics events began to collect a modest assortment of medals in long-distance running (courtesy of a world-record-breaking Kenyan) and weightlifting (via an octet of Bulgarians), all without a hint of embarrassment.

Such an approach embodies the current philosophy at work in both Qatar and Dubai in terms of nation building: money spent in the right places can solve any problem. "If we can't do it ourselves, pay someone from outside to do it" seems to be the motto, though this has not always yielded the best results. Qatar attempted to create a prestigious football league by using vast sums of money to tempt experienced (others might say washed-up) footballers to Doha. The Brazilian World Cup winner Romario lasted only a few months before fleeing back to the beaches of Rio. When the Qataris then began scouting the world for talent to play for the national team, the governing body of world football had to intervene and issue new directives regarding eligibility and citizenship. Otherwise Qatar would have fielded a team of 10 Brazilians (even they weren't that desperate for a goalkeeper) during a World Cup qualifying campaign. Anthro-apologists argue that such an approach is reflective of the fact that slavery was still practiced in much of the Arabian Peninsula up until the 1960s. Thus Qatar is simply applying a more ancient emperor–gladiator dynamic to international football. Since the national team is as much a reflection of the leader as the people he rules, why not spend some money and get some players who know what they're doing?

At times like this you also realize that despite the flags and national anthems, the foundations of many Gulf states are still relatively young. Until the end of the First World War, modern-day Iraq and Saudi Arabia would both have been dependencies of the Ottoman Empire. As of yet, their citizens have not reached (or been allowed to reach) a definitive consensus on ideas such as nationhood and identity. If the nation is not clearly defined, the concept of citizenship must be equally fluid. About 6,000 people belonging to one Qatari tribe had their citizenship revoked over claims that they also held Saudi citizenship. The "real" reason for this action was supposed to be that some members of the tribe were plotters in a failed coup attempt. Just like the region's infrastructure, the issue of nationality remains under construction.

Anyway, in much of the Middle East the idea of swearing allegiance to a flag or a country is still a subjective process. In actuality, loyal citizens swear fealty not just to the nation, but to a man and his extended family, be they Al Maktoums, Al Sauds, Al Nahyans, Al Sabahs, or even Al Tikritis. Your fortunes rise and fall with those to whom you pledge allegiance. Even *coups d'état* are as often as not family affairs – kinsfolk feuding over rank, position, and entitlements, rather than real changes in political structure. Loyalties are often expressed on a much smaller scale, to one's family and by extension to one's *qabila* or tribe. This point was borne out when I inadvertently gave Khamees the Norman Tebbit Sporting Loyalty Test. The former British government minister once caused a ruckus when he castigated British-born Asians for supporting either the Indian or Pakistani cricket teams rather than England. Khamees admitted that if the choice were available, he'd prefer to play up front for Dubai than for the UAE, his supposed homeland.

Iraq is one country in the Middle East that has attempted to break this mold by replacing the hereditary monarchies such as in Dubai. Yet in its attempt to do so, it had ended up smashing the family china to smithereens. After the King of Iraq was ousted in 1958 (admittedly his father had ruled half of modern-day Saudi Arabia and he shouldn't have been given the job by the British in the first place), the monarchy was replaced by a republic. But over time, the country morphed into a nightmarish tribal dictatorship under the leadership of a selected few individuals from Saddam Hussein's home town of Tikrit. The result of this political deviance over the years has been well documented, leaving somewhere like Dubai an attractive berth for Iraqis caught up in the raging storm that is their nation's struggle with history.

Although low-rent Sharjah hosts the largest Iraqi community in the UAE, there is a good selection of Iraqi restaurants in Dubai that serve traditional favorites such as *gutan* and *masgoof*, a whole fish cooked to perfection while propped up in front of a wood fire. Sitting down to lunch one day in just such an establishment, I learned that my waiter was a Sunni Muslim from Baghdad forced to flee his homeland. His reason was straightforward. "Someone wants to kill me," he said. A medical professional by training, finding a suitable job in Dubai was proving difficult. "I was a doctor, now I cook fish," he added with a shrug. You could tell that it hurt. When my meal finally arrived after a lengthy wait, there was a problem. I had inadvertently ordered an entire fish – an oversized meal large to enough to feed three people, and costing nearly triple what I had planned to spend. A little like the Americans in Iraq, my lack of familiarity with the local environment had given me a lot more than I had bargained for.

A roar from the crowd signaled the start of the second half. Prior to the game, much had been made of the composition of the Iraqi team. While sectarian strife was exploding back home, this combination of Shiites, Sunnis, and Kurds was heralded as a beacon of hope. Although Saudi Arabia and Iran constitute the powerhouses of Middle East football, with each passing minute the underdog Iraqis began to grow in confidence.

When a goal finally comes, it's a crowd pleaser. The Iraqi captain meets a corner kick at the far post with a well-placed header back across the goal. As the net billows from the impact of the ball, a millisecond of disbelief is followed by a huge roar. Pandemonium ensues. The jubilant Iraqis around me can't believe it. The last ten minutes are spent with their heads in their hands, imploring the referee to blow time. Despite a few near misses at the other end, this single goal proves enough and joy is unbounded when the whistle finally goes. The men around me become teary-eyed as the television commentator loses the run of himself, Brazilian style, to a frantic echoing refrain of *alf alf mabrook Iraq, alf alf mabrook Iraq* – a thousand thousand blessings, a thousand thousand blessings.

Although that arabic phrase *mabrook* (you are blessed) is commonly heard across the Arab world, Dubai has always preferred to live by an Irish adage: "God helps those who help themselves." And as someone who has lived for such a long time in the Middle East, I was surprised by how little mention I heard of the most potent word in much of the Arabian Gulf: *wasta*. Vitamin W, pull, connections: these are all possible translations and euphemisms, none of which really does the term justice. *Wasta* in this case means influence, often due to family connections, which is a vital ingredient in any successful Arabian enterprise. Yet throughout my time exploring Dubai, there was a sense of confidence that things could go well without having some longstanding family association to sort everything out for you. These feelings of self-reliance and possibility are both infectious and magnetic. Dubai has lured professionals and entrepreneurs from across the Arab world looking for a life denied to them in Lebanon, Jordan, Syria, or Iraq. Though an accountant from Amman may have to put up with a token Emirati "boss" with considerably less education and experience, the salary and working conditions usually compensate for the inequity.

In the past, Dubai had no love affair with other Arab states. Whereas millions of Arabs from the region's poorer nations are found working across other Gulf countries, Dubai has been happier to rely on immigrants from the Indian subcontinent. In fact the emirate had a rather sour experience with Arab school teachers from Syria, Egypt, and Iraq during the 1950s and 1960s. Along with teaching local children 1 + 1 = 2, some also began preaching Soviet-inspired Pan-Arab unity and socialism. The Maktoums didn't take kindly to being labeled imperial lackeys beholden to British colonial masters and quickly got rid of those responsible. Since then, the number of Arab expatriates has remained at relatively low levels. Although a contentious issue, some argue that this approach has actually benefited Dubai. In other Gulf states such as Kuwait, the local population accuse expatriate Egyptians of ruining their country by importing an all-pervasive culture of cronyism and corruption from their home nation. Maybe Dubai has escaped this mythical Mummy's Curse?

Nevertheless, even this narrative is changing. A local Emirati man put it best, explaining over dinner how Dubai benefits from the endemic corruption present in other Arab countries: "Dubai attracts the best Arabs from across the region. It gives them a place to excel, opportunities that are denied to them in their own country, due to *wasta* and corruption. The Europeans and Americans will come and go but the Arabs will stay. The people coming now are the Arabs we need." My source even said that Dubai's relatively high cost of living was a natural filter separating the wheat from the chaff. As far as he was concerned, if people wanted to live as cheaply as possible, remit all their savings back home, and were happy to work in a system where *wasta* and sycophancy were the order of the day, they could go to Saudi Arabia.

For someone who has not lived in the Gulf, it is hard to explain exactly how restrictive business opportunities can be for both local people and expats. This part of the world can be the ultimate closed shop and companies exert considerable time and effort simply keeping competitors out. As most Middle East economies are run through a system of exclusive licenses, behind-the-scenes manipulation, bribery, oligopoly, opaque government practices, and cronyism, a sense of hopelessness often pervades potential entrepreneurs, especially those who do not have *wasta* and come from "unconnected" families. Robert Fisk commented on the issue of family power in the region in his book *Pity the Nation*: "For Lebanon was run by *zaim*, the 'leaders', the powerful feudal chieftains whom the Lebanese would describe as 'honoured families' but whom the average Westerner would quickly identify as Mafiosi." Dubai appeals to Arabs born outside of these "honoured families," who can control all avenues of advancement.

Maybe this was one of the secrets behind the Dubai dream. Members of the Maktoum family certainly hold top positions across the emirate, but one got the feeling that sheer incompetence is not as blatantly rewarded (or excused) simply because of family or tribal loyalties as it can be elsewhere in the region. One of the architects of the Dubai dream was Sultan Ahmad Bin Sulayem. A civil servant, he rose through the ranks to assume a number of top positions. But even *The Times* of London had a hard time grasping this fact, continually referring to him in a profile as "the Sultan," assuming that a man in such a powerful position would have to be royalty.

In a random encounter in a gift shop in an Italian-themed mall in Jumeirah, a Yemeni shopkeeper sang the city's praises unprompted but with fervor: "If you come to Dubai and start a business, in two years you will be rich." It sounded like gold-rush talk to me, but in the minds of many Arabs, Dubai has found an answer to the *wasta* equation.

Dubai is also an equal opportunity bolthole. Not only does it welcome Iraqi refugees fleeing bullets or Syrian professionals pursuing careers, it pulls up a chair for other international émigrés in need of sanctuary in today's security-conscious world. And given its location, Dubai will never be short of takers. If you stick a compass in a map and draw a circle with Dubai as the epicenter, you quickly see why. With neighbors such as Saudi Arabia, Sudan, Somalia, Iraq, Iran, Afghanistan, and Pakistan, all rife with internal conflict, revolutionaries, separatist militias, military dictatorships, political assassinations, suicide bombers, messianic religious leaders, and weapons of mass destruction (both real and imaginary), there will always be a need for a safe haven.

Of all the stories I heard in Dubai, none encapsulated the appeal of the city more than a conversation I had while sitting in traffic in the Shindagha Tunnel. My taxi driver was of course a Pakistani, from the Waziristan tribal area bordering Afghanistan. As we talked about his homeland, he told me he hadn't been home in three years. He was afraid of being press-ganged into fighting for the Taliban against the American military. Due to a seemingly non-retractable *mi casa es tu casa* invitation offered by some of his kinfolk to a certain Saudi gentleman, his hometown had been turned into a war zone. My driver also gave me a breakdown of the secondhand weapons market in his home town: a rocket-propelled grenade launcher cost only 3,000 dirhams (US$810), while a Kalashnikov could be had for a few hundred. Overall, he preferred Dubai.

But it's not only taxi drivers who find sanctuary here. Dubai is also popular with the aristocrats of the global expat community: political leaders who have tumbled from grace. Former Pakistani Prime Minister Benazir Bhutto found safety in a gilded exile in Dubai after she fell from power. A failed assassination attempt welcomed her arrival home, followed by a more successful one soon after. Be it postcolonial political turmoil in Sub-Saharan Africa or conflict over the control of natural resources in Central

Asia, the rich and powerful of these regions find in Dubai something that no amount of money can buy at home: peace of mind. If behind every great fortune there is a crime, this can be doubly so in "emerging markets," especially when your enemies may possess both the motivation and the wherewithal to part you from your hard-earned cash – and your life. The knowledge that everything could be taken from you at a moment's notice leads many an oligarch, former head of state, or warlord to search for a refuge for themselves and their money.

This is where Dubai steps in. Buying a property gets the owner a 99-year residency visa, a bank account free of outside interference, and a second home to run to if or when things turn sour. Thus, paying over the odds for a hurriedly built villa that comes with such benefits can seem like a bargain. This is the point that many western analysts never truly grasp about Dubai, as they continually compare it to the likes of New York, London, and Hong Kong. Up against these long-established centers of power, Dubai will always come out second best. But when compared to some of the least progressive republics of the former Soviet Union, or certain ruinous economies across Africa and Asia, it can look like paradise.

Yet Dubai has an inverse and parasitical relationship with its neighbors. The worse the regional situation gets, the better things are for Dubai. The Iraqi invasion of Kuwait in 1990, followed by the slow death of an unpredictable Saddam Hussein regime, was a boon for the city. Kuwaitis who were reluctant to invest their money at home (after the mass pillaging conducted by the departing Iraqis in 1991) invested in Dubai instead. However, this is a dangerous environment; carcinogens can silently infiltrate the body only to reveal themselves when the damage is terminal. While tens of thousands of dovish Pakistanis live and work in Dubai, there is no doubting that Al-Qaeda and Taliban sympathizers (both locals and foreigners) live there as well. One of the 9-11 attackers hailed from nearby Ras Al Khaimah, and the UAE was one of only three countries that recognized the Taliban's short-lived Islamic Emirate of Afghanistan.

During its brief term in office, the Taliban used Dubai as both a logistical and a financial center when dealing with the outside world. Is it due to these close links that Dubai has not yet experienced any Al-Qaeda-inspired blowback, notwithstanding its reputation for un-Islamic licentiousness? The city is also a willing home to the United States Navy and a group calling itself the Al-Qaeda Organization in the Emirates and Oman has threatened violence if all American military bases in the UAE are not dismantled. There have been *jihadi* bombings and shootings in Saudi Arabia, Kuwait, and Qatar, but Dubai and the rest of the UAE have remained untouched. Being a center of calm in the eye of a raging storm has sparked a range of conspiracy theories.

The most common is that the global *jihadi* network has chosen not to piss in its own backyard. Much of the US$500,000 used to fund the 9-11 attacks was transferred through Dubai. The city is also a focal point for the unregulated *hawala* money transfer system, which is used to send money around the world anonymously. *Hawala* accounts for up to US$20 billion of transfers and is used by legitimate businessmen and ordinary people from Africa and Asia, and groups who prefer to operate in the shadows can easily transfer funds within this system without causing suspicion. Although only the most hardened conspiracy theorist would try to argue that the powers that be in Dubai actively support terrorism, one specialist in the field has accused the city of "wilful blindness" when it comes to shady money transiting through the city. In the wake of a US government report highlighting the "Dubai Connection" in the 9-11 attacks, the local authorities were very keen to be seen as partners in the fight against the finance networks employed by groups such as Al-Qaeda. However, given that Dubai has a deeply entrenched laissez-faire policy toward the movement of money, any attempts to curb the free-wheeling movement of cash were always going to be cosmetic.

Dubai's deep ties to Afghanistan (even warlords need a break) have also made it a staging post for a new kind of money laundering. Referred to as a narco-commodity exchange, this is a system whereby Afghani opium is exchanged not for money but for large quantities of commercial goods. These can then be sold legally, which gives the seller the appearance of owning a legitimate business. Rather than receiving a suitcase of money or a large bank transfer, a container of auto parts or color televisions (shipped from or through Dubai) generates considerably less attention.

There have also been whispered rumors that some high-ranking UAE officials have always been sympathetic to the Al-Qaeda cause. Speculation remains that members of Abu Dhabi's ruling family may have received a visit from Osama Bin Laden during a hunting trip in Afghanistan in 1999. Insider accounts have claimed that US intelligence services were contemplating a missile strike to kill Bin Laden, but were afraid of taking out a cluster of Abu Dhabi sheikhs in the process. Then there are the theories that Al-Qaeda has been paid off not to mess around in the UAE, or that the authorities in Dubai and Abu Dhabi have agreed to turn a blind eye to any comings and goings so long as no attacks occur on Emirati soil.

Over time, I developed a suitably far-fetched conspiracy theory of my own. What would happen if Al-Qaeda were to launch a major attack in Dubai? After the initial outcry, people would demand action. What if police eventually traced the attackers back to the Al-Qaeda and Taliban strongholds along the border between Afghanistan and Pakistan? Dubai's Pathan population from these tribal areas might be blamed and heads would have to roll. This could be followed by mass expulsions and an embargo on any new workers coming to Dubai from Pakistan. Mothers and children would no longer receive the hundreds of dollars they need to survive each month, wired home from their husbands working in Dubai. And arriving back in the villages outside Peshawar would be thousands of extremely pissed-off tribesmen with a serious ax to grind (and remember, an AK-47 only costs a couple of hundred dirhams) with those responsible for them losing their livelihoods back in Dubai. Al-Qaeda wouldn't stand a chance, and it probably knows that.

Exactly what the local chapter of the Al-Qaeda Organization in the Emirates and Oman would make of a hallowed Dubai institution such as St. Mary's Church is anyone's guess. But just like everywhere else in the city, it was suffering from severe congestion. Squeezing past the crowds gathered in the doorway one Friday morning, I made my way inside and stood at the back of the congregation. The parishioners constituted a multitude of nationalities, though without doubt India and the Philippines occupied the gold and silver medal positions respectively.

In Islamic theology, the Judaic-Christian religions are supposed to enjoy a somewhat privileged position compared to other faiths. Muslims are compelled to believe that Jesus (Essa) and Abraham (Ibrahim) are Prophets of

God. Christians and Jews are referred to as *ahl al kitab* (People of the Book) and are seen to believe in the same God as that worshiped in Islam – though without the corrective addenda that the Koran gives those two faiths. Although it contains many ecumenical verses, there are others chiding both Christians and Jews for not embracing Islam and air-brushing the Prophet Mohammed from their holy books:

> *O people of the Book! Why do you disbelieve in the Ayat [the verses about Prophet Mohammed present in the Torah and the Gospel] while you bear witness to the truth?*
> *O people of the Book: Why do you mix truth with falsehood and conceal the truth while you know?*
>   Koran, Sura 3, Verses 70–71

Like everything else in this world, it's all a matter of interpretation.

Dubai's tolerance is in marked contrast to the Kingdom of Saudi Arabia, where churches are not allowed, despite the fact that Christians are supposedly members of an exclusive club. Christians in search of communal prayer have to gather behind closed doors. A Filipino friend who worked for the all-powerful Saudi Aramco recalled how the oil company hid the fact that it hired ministers and priests to attend to the spiritual needs of its expat employees on its secluded compounds. Men of the cloth were identified as "counselors" or "social workers" instead. Just as the presence of Hindu temples makes Dubai a more attractive destination for Non-Resident Indians, the same religious freedom makes it an attractive posting for Christians from across Asia. In particular, Dubai has become a sanctuary for a small number of Pakistanis of the Christian persuasion, whose churches have been occasionally attacked by Islamic fundamentalists. This lingering possibility of violence is difficult for many to live with. One Christian man from Lahore told me that he and his wife had simply had enough and left.

However, the authorities in Dubai do not always acknowledge their tolerance. In order to avoid censure from its less tolerant Arab neighbors, the official policy in the UAE (as in much of the Arab world) is that Israeli citizens are not allowed to enter the country. In reality, Dubai is happy to pay lip service to the "No Israeli Left Behind" policy while allowing Israelis to do business discreetly in the city. Although websites with a potentially Zionist .il extension are blocked, having an Israeli stamp in your passport does not disqualify you from entering the country, as is the case elsewhere in the Middle East. The Syrian and Lebanese border officials who inspect every page of your passport in Damascus and Beirut insist that they aren't looking for anything in particular, but it's no secret that they're seeking proof that you've been to Israel.

The true extent of the difference between Dubai and the rest of the Arab world really rang home one day when a salesman in a shopping mall nonchalantly told me he was Jewish. It is unusual for people of the Judaic faith to announce their religious affiliation openly to strangers in the Middle East. Yet this is one area where Dubai prefers to adopt a low-key approach. When a major takeover deal planned by a Dubai-based company fell through in the US amid security fears and criticism that the UAE often refuses visas to Israelis, the Dubai authorities could have cited numerous examples where they had simply ignored this ban. But then they might have drawn scorn from their Arab brethren and upset such notable outfits as the Al-Qaeda Organization in the Emirates and Oman. Tightrope walking is a skill that all Middle Eastern enterprises must learn in order to be successful.

And vigilance will always be necessary. Dubai is encircled by nations where religion is often used as a fuel to fan political turmoil and sectarian violence, yet it has been inoculated against such strife so far. This is testament to the fact that in Dubai, regional expectations frequently get turned on their heads. Again and again Dubai has gone against perceived wisdom and looked to the future with optimism when many people only see storm clouds on the horizon.

While such thoughts were no doubt far from the minds of the people celebrating mass that day in St. Mary's, the first reading from the Book of Amos contained a caution against complacency that would, with hindsight, prove most portentous. It warned of the evils of excess and reminded the congregation to bear in mind the ruin of Joseph, the retribution that awaits when reverence for the divine is lost – wealth is worshiped for its own sake and prosperity is limited to a select few:

> *Woe to those ensconced so snugly in Zion and to those who feel safe on the mountain of Samaria. Lying on ivory beds and sprawling on their divans, they dine on lambs from the flock, and stall-fattened veal; they bawl to the sound of the harp, they invent new instruments of music like David, they drink wine by the bowlful. And use the finest oil for anointing themselves but about the ruin of Joseph they do not care at all. That is why they will be the first to be exiled; the sprawlers' revelry is over.*

The Old Testament always was a bit of a killjoy.

16

Last Orders

THE BURJ AL ARAB HOTEL is without doubt the corporate logo of the Dubai dream. Instantly recognizable, this spinnaker-shaped hotel is a global phenomenon. It appears on just about every souvenir the city has to offer, an icon immediately associated with wealth and ambition. Architecturally, it's magnificent. You would have to be an inveterate architectural Salafist not to appreciate the way the exterior cuts away, like a ship's sail caught in a burst of wind, snapping the synapses of your brain to attention. Even if not a single guest had ever stayed in its US$10,000-a-night suites, the Burj Al Arab would still have paid for itself. The publicity it generated was unquantifiable. This is what put Dubai on the map.

I had been avoiding it until now. To start with the city's most prominent landmark had seemed both unimaginative and trite. But as my time in Dubai neared an end, this was an omission that had to be addressed. As is often the way, a friend arriving from out of town was the catalyst to visit some of the tourist sites I had missed so far. First were the Iranian wind towers of Bastakiyah, followed by a walk through the pre-oil heritage haven of Shindagha. From there it was across the creek by *abra* to the spice and gold *souks* of Deira. By the end of the day, the lack of modernity was almost embarrassing. Dubai was supposed to be a kingdom of bling, yet there was a distinct shortage of ostentation on the whistle-stop tour we had just conducted. Thankfully, a reservation for drinks at the Burj Al Arab was at hand.

Completed in 1997, the Burj Al Arab was the city's first attempt to redefine itself in the modern age. Other projects have followed such as the 800-meter-plus Burj Dubai that were taller, bigger, more expensive, more ambitious, but this is without doubt the one that was still the most emblematic. The Burj Al Arab was Dubai's first run at architectural enchantment and given the hectic pace of development, it was practically middle-aged. The interior décor failed to match the high standards set on the exterior; as with so many things here, it's what you see on the outside that counts. Upstairs in the Skybar, the lighting seemed to have been culled from the set of an old *Doctor Who* episode. Round spheres of primary colors – red, blue, and yellow – waxed and waned eerily on the tables and overhead. In the lobby, the gold paint on the coffee tables had faded, exposing patches of bare wood beneath; while a candy-striped carpet of yellow and orange squiggles would have given a connoisseur of traditional Bedouin weaving an epileptic fit. Even so, a little Las Vegas kitsch is not in itself a hanging offense.

Since building the Burj Al Arab, the designers behind the next stages of the Dubai dream had allowed a lot more of Arabia to seep into their minds. Just next door, two more five-star hotels had been built in Madinat Jumeirah, paying homage to all things Arabian, both inside and out. The hotels were even linked together by miniature *abras*, with a "traditional" *souk* located in the middle. Rather than crossing the real Creek to the real *souks* in a real *abra*, the busy tourist can now do it all in miniature, without leaving the confines of their hotel complex. In a way, this is the perfect summation of the Dubai model, a five-star air-conditioned re-creation of the real thing.

While the seafaring theme of the Burj Al Arab's exterior pays homage to an element of Dubai's past, if you're looking for a taste of the local Arab culture, you had better settle for the coffee. As we took in the unexpectedly psychedelic swirls of the lobby, a man dressed in a traditional white robe approached us bearing a long-spouted coffee pot, a gesture of hospitality incumbent on every conscientious host in Arabia. With his left hand he barely covered the bottom of each *finjan* (the small, handle-less cups used to serve traditional Arabic coffee) and waited for us to drink. If you are a stickler for etiquette, accept two or three refills fairly sharpish, before gently rocking the cup from side to side to indicate you have had enough.

Once you stray outside the mosque, there is nothing more indicative of Arabia than the customs and tradition wrapped up in the serving and drinking of this bitter golden tipple. It is served at every event of importance: weddings, funerals, political rallies. In this age-old tradition, so many of the region's social conventions are subtly on display – all you have to do is watch and learn. You see the premium that is placed on formality and ritual: don't put the cup on the table as this is deemed an insult to the server. You see the deference that is paid to age: in the absence of a *muqahwa* (coffee server) the youngest person should stand and serve the others. You also see the importance of social status and position: the person occupying the most senior rank should be served first.

Yet on this particular day the spell didn't last for long. In Dubai, the specter of questionable authenticity is never far away. We quickly learned that the *muqahwa* was in fact from Syria. The symbolism and the theater that surround the Gulf coffee ritual could have been just as alien to him. In Syria, Arabic coffee is even a different color, sooty black instead of grayish yellow. As we drank our coffee, my friend asked if the Burj Al Arab really was a seven-star hotel, as is so often reported. The *muqahwa* replied that it was in fact a five-star hotel, "but we offer seven-star service!" This was a classic example of how Dubai is willing to let the truth be bent and encourages the media to indulge in its love of superlatives. There was no such thing as a seven-star hotel when the Burj Al Arab was built, but the tag stuck. And no one was going out of their way to dissuade the public otherwise. Whether or not this was a case of simulation or dissimulation has been lost in the ether. Yet the cynically minded could posit that Dubai's most iconic project was built on a lie.

Whereas most cities reveal themselves in a manner akin to a striptease, slowly removing the layers to reveal what lies underneath, in my eyes Dubai had followed an inverted ethnography. With every new experience, every encounter both planned and accidental, another layer of meaning was tipped into the ever-expanding landfill of my mind. Yet the multiplicity was at times too much. There were too many nationalities with different stories to tell. I often felt as if I was whirling around inside a cultural kaleidoscope, continually bombarded by meteorites of multiplicative meaning. Time and time again Dubai failed the most basic demographic definition of a nation: the same people living in the same place. This was a place where concepts such as citizenship and nationality were skewed and defied one's expectations. There was also a lingering sense that while Dubai was miles wide, it was only an inch deep. And I sometimes feared that my own portrait would suffer accordingly.

Whenever I felt overwhelmed, it was best to return to first principles. Notwithstanding their scarcity, I knew that it was in the company of local people that a resolution awaited. But I had to be aware of imitations. The Syrian pouring coffee in the Burj Al Arab hadn't been the only time someone wearing a *kandura* had revealed himself to be anything but local.

Despite the relative paucity of citizens, meeting locals was never that difficult, once you made a conscious decision to do so. In practical terms, it involved making the most of every opportunity that came along. All you had to do was take the first step and let their natural gregariousness and hospitality take over. On many occasions after striking up a random conversation with a stranger in a bar or café, I would discover (only after they had left) that they had surreptitiously paid my bill.

As a rule, one must be careful when using the men met in bars across the Gulf as weathervanes from which to make generalizations about the local populace. It would be unsporting to employ the Saudi men – identifiable by the pointed collars and cufflinks of their white robes and their red-checked *gutras* – frequenting the bars in Deira to gain an insight into the Kingdom of Saudi Arabia. This method of ethnographic investigation generally doesn't allow the nationality in question to put its best foot forward. Imagine using the home crowd at a Millwall game as an exemplar of all things English. Such is the reputation acquired by many Gulf Arab visitors to Dubai that they can have trouble even getting a taxi after dark. One taxi driver explained how he never stopped for someone dressed in Arab robes if he could help it. He reasoned that a "local" would have his own car, so anyone dressed in a robe looking for a cab late at night would have to be a Saudi, Kuwaiti, or Qatari, generally in town to cut loose. "Too much trouble these people," he complained. "They get in the front seat, put their foot up here (pointing to the dashboard), change the radio station and turn it up full volume. Then at a red light, they change gear, put the car in 'Drive' and say, 'Go Baba! Go!'"

However, the locals I met one night in my preferred public house were much more restrained. Tareq, for example, wasn't a reveler intent on making crazy. He was an off-duty fireman having a pint and a game of pool on his way home from work. Dressed in a white collarless *kandura*, he didn't look like a pool shark, but he rushed around the table with an air of assurance. The long cord or *tarboosh* that hung from the neck of his robe down to his waist identified him as a citizen of the UAE; a much shorter *tarboosh* hanging from the shoulder is the Omani style. To avoid fouling the balls as he leaned over the table, he simply lifted the *tarboosh* and tucked it into his colorful headdress, which he wore whorled like a turban. This wraparound chic was currently all the rage with fashion-conscious younger men, as opposed to the regular flat *gutra* that older men drape over their heads. Once Tareq had given me a sound education in the art of pool, he was quick to buy me a drink in consolation. As we talked, he told me at length about his home town and the brotherly cantons in the rest of the UAE. While he understood a foreigner's desire to tour the other emirates, he reckoned that brevity was the best course of action once you stepped outside the confines of Dubai.

"I can spend one day in Al Ain and then I have to leave," he said, dismissing Abu Dhabi's second city with a wave of his hand. "There is nothing to do there. Don't think that the rest of the UAE is like Dubai. Dubai is special!" Unprompted, he was eager to tell me that Dubai's firefighting infrastructure was the best in the region, and that Saudis and others came there for training. The relaxed confidence with which he said these things was convincing and the more we talked, the more I wanted to believe Tariq's claims for Dubai. His optimism was a welcome relief from the negativity you often encounter once you start talking politics in the Middle East. When trying to predict future political events in the region, it's not that difficult to come over as a Solomon-like sage. All you have to do is choose the worst-case scenario and for much of the time you'll be right. Despite my natural inclination toward pessimism, Dubai's bubbly optimism had made me somewhat light-headed.

Although the emirate's political situation has much in common with its neighbors' - governed by hereditary potentates that brook no opposition - the hopefulness of men like Tareq was not uncommon. Despite its numerous detractors, expatriates with experience across the region also insist that Dubai is different. Even here in this bar, there were little pieces of evidence bearing witness to this claim. While there is no doubting that Dubai is a distinctly stratified society with a carefully established pecking order of privilege, it was refreshing to see a mixture of nationalities interacting with a tangible sense of respect: tapping the side of the pool table in appreciation of well-made shots and exchanging handshakes and pleasantries before and after each game. At the same time, Tareq wasn't about to give up his identity in this multicultural mêlée. Cultural inroads such as the wearing of western clothes held little appeal. "In Dubai we still wear the *kandura*. It is tradition. If I don't wear a *kandura*, my father gets angry," he joked. And on that point, he finished his drink and bade me goodnight.

Flush from this conversation, I moved from youth to experience and fell into conversation with two older local men sitting at the next table. Thankfully, Abdulrazzaq responded to my faltering Arabic in English, and we carried on a mishmash information exchange in two languages. One of the first questions he asked me was which Arab country I liked the best. This is a perennial question from competitive Gulf Arabs. I ran through a list in my head and settled on Oman for its natural beauty, but added that I would reserve judgment until I had visited Yemen. "Why do you want to go there?" he asked.

There were multiple reasons. Whenever I was feeling both arcadian and melodramatic, I pictured Yemen as the "Anti-Dubai," a place that had retained a singular identity in a rapidly changing, conjoined world. Yemen, as opposed to Dubai, was only millimeters wide in global terms, but I imagined it possessing a culture that was kilometers deep. In no state of mind to give accurate voice to these feelings, I made do with quoting an aphorism of the Prophet Mohammed learned from an encyclopedic Somalilander: "*al Hikmah Yemeniya*" (wisdom is Yemeni). This brought a huge grin from Abdulrazzaq. "I am from Yemen!" he said. So much for thoughts of singularity.

Abdulrazzaq had moved to Dubai over thirty years before. As the UAE attempted to increase the size of its "local" population, he and many others like him had been granted citizenship. Although "first-generation" locals have little or no say in the political affairs of Dubai, the fringe benefits of citizenship are much better than those on offer back home in Yemen or Syria. Even with relative newcomers such as Abdulrazzaq, the rulers of Dubai are keeping their side of the unofficial social contract written into the fine print of all the Gulf sheikhdoms. The local population puts up with the idiosyncrasies of the ruling family, as long as the government provides a job for life, free healthcare, education, and housing.

I was now in a situation where the hospitality one encounters in the Gulf can be a little dangerous, as each time I reciprocated the drink Abdulrazzaq bought for me, he insisted on returning the favor. Over the next few hours we spoke of many things. He decried the many ills he saw across the Arab world and insisted that there was one over-arching problem with the region: Arab leaders do nothing for their people, think of the nation as their personal property, and were ultimately unworthy of the positions of power they held. These sentiments are not uncommon (though not always spoken publicly) across the Arab world and Abdulrazzaq was very dismissive of the various "petty kings" in the region. His criticisms echoed the epic pessimism you hear from many poets across the Middle East, who have given voice to the sufferings endured by so many Arab people at the hands of their leaders since the fall of the Ottoman Empire. In a poem simply entitled "The City," Iraqi poet Adulwahab Al Bayati created a metaphor for both his homeland and much of the wider Arab region:

> When the city undressed herself
> I saw in her sad eyes
> The shabbiness of the leaders, thieves and pawns
> I saw in her eyes
> The gallows, the prisons, and the incinerators,
> The sadness, the confusion, the smoke...
>
> I saw: the man of tomorrow...
> Clothed in sorrow and blackness
> The policemen, the sodomites, and the pimps
> Spitting in his eyes
> As he lay shackled.
> I saw in her sad eyes:
> The gardens of ashes
> Drowned in shadow and stillness.

Abdulrazzaq was quick to point out that Dubai did not fall into this category. For his exegesis, he proceeded to tell a rather convoluted story that he attributed to Sheikh Mohammed, when the future ruler was a student in England. I had a hard time following the details, but the moral of the tale seemed to focus on the importance of humility.

By the end of the night, our conversation had turned slapdash but spiritual. Although he agreed that we were both "people of the book," Abdulrazzaq had a hard time with the fact that Christians refuse to recognize Mohammed as a prophet. Seeing as Muslims believe in Jesus, surely Christians could simply return the compliment? Ultimately, he was more concerned with explaining what constituted a good Muslim, which for him essentially meant a good person. "Don't look at the beard and just going to the mosque five times a day as being a good Muslim. It is what a man does that makes him good. Some people go to the mosque praying for their own wishes or for money. This is no good. You should go to the mosque only to pray to God."

Then he suddenly changed the topic: "What will you do when you go back to your country?" Before I had a chance to answer, he jumped in with a reply of his own: "You will write a book! There was a British man, he was in their army but he came here and dressed like an Arab and talked like an Arab. He wrote a famous book about the Arabs. I think they called him Mubarak."

He was, of course, referring to Sir Wilfred. And this was a comforting link between the past and the present, a reassurance that there was some value in using the prism of the past to refract the light of the present day. It had been Thesiger's wish that *Arabian Sands* be translated into Arabic, to provide a written record of an antediluvian Arabia for the generation who would grow up after the discovery of oil. Although the places Thesiger had passed through had been utterly transformed, this was still a fascinating land to travel in, once you adjusted your expectations. But for the time being, I was more self-absorbed.

As we enjoyed a final drink, I took Abdulrazzaq's words as both a vindication and a blessing. The fact that locals are such a small minority in their home town had put a unique twist on any attempt to write a "national epic," and the reality that even "locals" can be "foreigners" was oddly reassuring. Dubai, unlike many other places, lends itself to description by alien voices – and to multiple dreams.

Epilogue: Cameos

"THE LITTLE SEA-PORT OF DUBAI" is the caption written below a black-and-white photograph that Thesiger took in the Old Souk in May 1948. And it was to the Creek that I always found myself returning, whenever the opportunity arose. Regardless of the season, there is a singular vitality to the blend of textures that occur along its banks. Sometimes I found myself sitting on an *abra* near that same *souk* late at night, ready for sleep, a divergent discord of thoughts running through my head, the smell of diesel lingering in the air as the boat idled in the water, the captain waiting for a full load before setting off for the other side. The boat would fill up slowly, the quorum of Indians, Pakistanis, and Afghans climbing aboard in ones and twos. By now, the shops in the *souk* would have closed and the accompanying daytime throngs dissipated into the night. The bustle of the day gave way to a different rhythm as we all made for home. Out on the water, the breeze blowing in from the Gulf was a blissful relief from the heat. The lights of the buildings across the way illuminated the evening, beckoning us toward them. But we would not be the only sea-borne traffic. For just as the ferry boats carry commuters back and forth across the Creek, cruise boats plow a perpendicular route laden with corporate entertainment and tourists. While we may share the same stretch of water, in truth we're worlds apart.

On one evening, halfway across one of the cruise boats passed by, so close I could see inside. While I sweated and embraced the humid night air, they were cosseted behind glass. Inside amid the air-conditioning and the Armani, it was a formal affair. But a couple had moved outside onto the deck. The man was dressed in a crisp white shirt, while beside him a striking blonde was well turned out in a sequined evening gown. The man had a video recorder in his hand and as we passed below them, my shipmates and I suddenly found ourselves promoted to background extras in his holiday video. While I understood the curiosity, it didn't sit well with me. There was something inequitable and faintly iniquitous about the interchange. What kind of reaction would my fellow passengers receive if they toured the London Underground on a damp Wednesday evening, videoing the locals on their way home from work?

In a few seconds, however, my mood lifted. As our two vessels passed each other, the man zoomed in for his close-up. But at that same moment, my fellow passengers whipped out an array of mobile phones and began taking their own photographs and video clips, clearly focusing their attention on his female companion. These two worlds intersected for only a few seconds, but in that fleet-ing concentration of time, there was Dubai: "a miniature cameo of the world we live in," to quote James Joyce, Ireland's greatest psychogeographer. Here was a place where disparate and multiple worlds existed side by side, but where fissures in your expectations continually erupted.

As the lights of Deira drew closer, I slipped into conver-sation with one of the amateur photographers beside me. Within moments, an invitation was proffered, a request that would necessitate a trip back across the Creek the fol-lowing day. I hesitated for a moment, but then quickly acquiesced, remembering that when presented with such an unexpected invitation, you rarely regret saying "Yes."

Author's Note

To respect the privacy of those concerned, the names of
practically all the people who appear in this book have
been changed. In the same spirit, some of the establishments mentioned have also been renamed. Yet travelers,
like soldiers, march on their stomachs, so vegetarians can
indeed dine on *thali* and Mysore *masala dosa* at the Shiv
Sagar restaurant (Jain preparations available) in Meena
Bazaar, while the carnivorously inclined may prefer the
Afghan Kebab House in Naif – long may its skewers keep
turning.

Al-Maktoum Rulers of Dubai

Maktoum bin Buti	1833–1852
Said bin Buti	1852–1859
Hasher bin Maktoum	1859–1886
Rashid bin Maktoum	1886–1894
Maktoum bin Hasher	1894–1906
Buti bin Suhail	1906–1912
Said bin Maktoum	1912–1958
Rashid bin Saeed	1958–1990
Maktoum bin Rashid	1990–2006
Mohammed bin Rashid	2006–present

Bibliography

Al Fahim, Mohammed (2006) *From Rags to Riches*, London: LCAS.

Al Qasimi, Sultan Mohammed (1986) *The Myth of Arab Piracy*, London: Croom Helm.

Burdett, Anita L.P. (ed.) (1990) *Records of Dubai 1761–1960, Vol. 4 1938–1945*, Cambridge: Archive Editions.

Buxani, Ram (2003) *Taking the High Road*, Dubai: Motivate.

Cassara, John A. (2006) *Hide and Seek: Intelligence, Law Enforcement, and the Stalled War on Terrorist Finance*, Dulles, VA: Potomac Books.

Davidson, Christopher M. (2008) *Dubai: The Vulnerability of Success*, London: Hurst & Co.

Davis, Mike (2006) "Fear and Money in Dubai," *New Left Review*, Sept–Oct.

Dickey, Christopher (1994) *Expats*, New York: Atlantic Monthly Press.

Graz, Liesl (1992) *The Turbulent Gulf*, London: IB Tauris.

Heard-Bey, Frauke (2004) *From Trucial States to United Arab Emirates*, Dubai: Motivate.

Mackintosh-Smith, Tim (2005) *The Hall of a Thousand Columns*, London: John Murray.

Raban, Jonathan (1983) *Arabia: Through the Looking Glass*, London: Flamingo.

Thesiger, Wilfred (1995) *Desert, Marsh and Mountain*, Dubai: Motivate.

Thesiger, Wilfred (2004) *Arabian Sands*, Dubai: Motivate.

Thomas, Bertram (1932) *Arabia Felix*, New York: Charles Scribner's Sons.

Toye, P.L. (ed.) (1993) *The Lower Gulf Islands: Abu Musa and the Tunbs, Vol. 1818–1887*, *Arabian Geopolitics Regional Documentary Studies*, Cambridge: Archive Editions.

Tuson, Penelope (ed.) (1990) *Records of the Emirates Primary Documents 1820–1958, Vols 8 & 9*, Cambridge: Archive Editions.

Acknowledgments

WHEN WRITING A BOOK SUCH AS THIS ONE, you are often utterly dependent on the goodwill, intelligence, and wit of others. I was fortunate enough to encounter an abundance of all three. In Dubai, I am indebted to many people whose company made this venture considerably more fruitful than it otherwise might have been. For a variety of reasons, however, it is better that many of these people remain nameless. That said, I would like to say *shukran* to the two participants in the "Liwa Conference" for shedding light on the more opaque aspects of Dubai Inc. and cheers to Secret Dubai for her sterling work and snappy songs. I must also thank Lincoln for shining a light into some of Dubai's less well-publicized corners, while I should add a *mamnoun* to Mohammed for his warmth and welcome and a *namaste* to Abhi and his family for their kindness. And I would like to thank the following for taking the time to share their experience and expertise on a number of matters: Christopher Davidson, John Cassara, Ram Buxani, Patrick Chichester, and Mohammed Hareb.

In London, my gratitude goes to Nick and Sally for their editorial guidance and patience. I would also like to include a particular thank-you to Erika Heilman. In Kuwait, I'd like to thank Abdi, Bronnie, Doug, Emerson, Lorie, Norma, Jim, Virginia, Sean, and Vas for their encouragement and hospitality over the years. I'd like to add a special thank-you to Tony for his assiduous and timely expatiations on the final manuscript. In Florida, I'd like to thank Paul, Lisa, and Sharon for putting real meaning into the phrase "a home from home."

In Ireland, my thanks to all members (current, former, and associated) of Galway's Flat Line Society for their encouragement from afar. Closer to home, I'd like to thank my parents, J.T. and Mary, for so many things it would be impossible to list them all here. I also want to thank my two brothers: Richard for providing a welcoming retreat in Dublin on so many occasions; and Gerard for seeing three chapters where there was one – his expertise was simply indispensible.

Finally, my deepest gratitude goes to Roxanne, to whom this book is dedicated, for faith, love, and belief.